# NO WORRIES

## LEARNING TO TRUST OUR SOVEREIGN GOD

*A **Flexible** Inductive Bible Study*

BY JAN SILVIOUS AND PAM GILLASPIE

**No Worries: Learning to Trust Our
Sovereign God**

Copyright © 2014 by Pam Gillaspie and
Jan Silvious
Published by Precept Ministries
International
P.O. Box 182218
Chattanooga, Tennessee 37422
www.precept.org

ISBN: 978-1-62119-227-5

## Dedication . . .

To worriers and recovering worriers everywhere.

## Acknowledgements

Many thanks to the editorial and marketing teams at Precept, to the class at
Immanuel Church who piloted this material, and to our families for bearing with us
during the writing and editing process.

# NO WORRIES
Learning to Trust Our Sovereign God

# No Worries

## LEARNING TO TRUST OUR SOVEREIGN GOD

There is nothing quite like your favorite pair of jeans. You can dress them up, you can dress them down. You can work in them, play in them, shop in them . . . live in them. They always feel right. It is my hope that the structure of this Bible study will fit you like those jeans; that it will work with your life right now, right where you are whether you're new to this whole Bible thing or whether you've been studying the Book for years!

How is this even possible? Smoke and mirrors, perhaps? The new mercilessly thrown in the deep end? The experienced given pompoms and the job of simply cheering others on? None of the above.

*No Worries: Learning to Trust our Sovereign God* is a flexible Bible study—designed with options that allow you to go as deep each week as you choose. If you're just starting out and feeling a little overwhelmed, stick with the main text and don't think a second thought about the sidebar assignments. If you're looking for a challenge, then take the sidebar prompts and dig with vigor! As you move along through the study, think of the sidebars and "Digging Deeper" boxes as that 2% of lycra you find in certain jeans . . . the wiggle-room that will help them fit just right.

Life has a way of ebbing and flowing and this study is designed to ebb and flow right along with it!

**Enjoy!**

# How to use this study

Flexible inductive Bible studies meet you where you are and take you as far as you want to go.

**1. WEEKLY STUDY:** The main text guides you through the complete topic of study for the week.

**2. FYI boxes:** For Your Information boxes provide bite-sized material to shed additional light on the topic.

**3. ONE STEP FURTHER and other sidebar boxes:** Sidebar boxes give you the option to push yourself a little further. If you have extra time or are looking for an extra challenge, you can try one, all, or any number in between! These boxes give you the ultimate in flexibility.

## ONE STEP FURTHER:

**Word Study: *torah*/law**
The first of eight Hebrew key words we encounter for God's Word is *torah* translated "law." If you're up for a challenge this week, do a word study to learn what you can about *torah*. Run a concordance search and examine where the word *torah* appears in the Old Testament and see what you can learn about it from the contexts.

If you decide to look for the word for "law" in the New Testament, you'll find that the primary Greek word is *nomos*.

Be sure to see what Paul says about the law in Galatians 3 and what Jesus says in Matthew 5.

**4. DIGGING DEEPER boxes:** If you're looking to go further, Digging Deeper sections will help you sharpen your skills as you continue to mine the truths of Scripture for yourself.

## Digging Deeper

**What else does God's Word say about counselors?**

If you can, spend some time this week digging around for what God's Word says about counselors.

Start by considering what you already know about counsel from the Word of God and see if you can show where these truths are in the Bible. Make sure that the Word says what you think it says.

# NO WORRIES
Learning to Trust Our Sovereign God

## The Sin We Excuse

*And who of you by being worried can add a*
*single hour to his life?*
–Matthew 6:27

Relativism. Tolerance. When nothing is wrong, everything is right and "right" is meaningless.

When "nothing is wrong" and what the Bible calls sin carries the day, damage follows. In our current cultural fray our attention usually turns to societal hot buttons—homosexual behavior and relationships, beginning of life and end of life issues. Moral issues. Issues of life and sex and right and wrong. It's funny, though, that while we can be so sure of the negative outcomes of certain behaviors, there are others we turn a blind eye to. Often, while calling others to fight their predisposition to sin we pass over our own. Over the course of the next eight weeks we're going to look at what God's Word has to say about one of the more acceptable sins of our time—worry. Not only is worry acceptable, if we're going to be honest, some of us view it (or have viewed it) as a virtue that demonstrates our responsibility, caring, and love when in fact it is only a cheap knock-off.

We could easily spend the next weeks spinning yarns and telling tales of worry in our personal lives that would be mildly entertaining and somewhat instructive—and we will share a few. Our focus, however, will be on what God's Word says about worry and how we can combat this socially acceptable, yet strangling sin in our lives. As we study, we'll look at specific passages in Scripture that talk about worry but we'll also look across the pages of God's Word to see how worry plays out in the lives of biblical characters and consider what we can learn from both their failures and successes along the way.

No Worries
Learning to Trust Our Sovereign God

3

**Worry that Spans the Ages**

Worry can affect us at any age. Children often worry about things that feel way too big to handle in their minds.

I can remember as a twelve year old worrying about my mother not arriving to sit with me in church. I don't know where I thought she was. She taught a class, so often she was late coming into the service. I felt anxiety rising in my throat when the music began. In my mind I became an abandoned orphan who would have no one to care for and comfort me. I know that sounds really far fetched but that's what happens when worry takes over. The harmless becomes horrible and the meaningless becomes monstrous. Of course, that was when I was a child. "Children are good observers but poor interpreters."

Then, I became an adult. I still worried about things. They just got bigger. When I was twenty-five or so, I didn't worry about being abandoned but I began to worry about dying and leaving my own children. Who would raise them? Who could care for them like I did? And who would? Worry, worry, worry. It was eating away at me.

In fact it was my worry that ultimately caused me to get serious about a relationship with the Lord. The first time I heard Kay Arthur speak I heard her say, "If I live praise the Lord, if I die, praise the Lord. If I live or die, praise the Lord." I wondered how on earth anyone could say that but I knew I wanted to be able to say the same thing.

Maybe you have longed to be able to say "Whatever happens, praise the Lord!" If so, I understand; but this much I know . . . "being worried cannot add a single hour" to your life.

# CONSIDER the WAY you THINK

What do you worry about?

Do you classify yourself as a person who occasionally worries or as a "worrier"?

Can you remember a time when you didn't worry?

Are you aware of anything that set it off?

Describe your view of the Bible. (Do you believe it is God's Word? Do you believe it is authoritative? Why/why not?)

Describe your view of God. (Do you believe God is sovereign? Do you believe He is omniscient? Do you believe He is good? Explain your reasoning.)

NO WORRIES
Learning to Trust Our Sovereign God

*Notes*

## OBSERVE the TEXT of SCRIPTURE

While Jesus often spoke in parables, He never beat around the bush. In fact, some of His most straight-forward teaching on the topic of worry comes in what is often referred to as the Sermon on the Mount. Matthew records this teaching in chapters 5 through 7 of his Gospel. Jesus' teaching on worry appears right in the middle of Matthew 6. Although we'll circle back to this text in more depth in later weeks, today let's take a summary look at Matthew 6 section by section.

## SETTING the SCENE

Jesus speaks to a crowd on a mountainside somewhere on the Sea of Galilee in the northern part of Israel.

**READ** Matthew 6:1-15. **MARK** every reference to different groups of people (e.g. *men, hypocrites*, etc.) in a distinctive way.

### Matthew 6:1-15

1  *"Beware of practicing your righteousness before men to be noticed by them; otherwise you have no reward with your Father who is in heaven.*

2  *"So when you give to the poor, do not sound a trumpet before you, as the hypocrites do in the synagogues and in the streets, so that they may be honored by men. Truly I say to you, they have their reward in full.*

3  *"But when you give to the poor, do not let your left hand know what your right hand is doing,*

4  *so that your giving will be in secret; and your Father who sees what is done in secret will reward you.*

5  *"When you pray, you are not to be like the hypocrites; for they love to stand and pray in the synagogues and on the street corners so that they may be seen by men. Truly I say to you, they have their reward in full.*

6  *"But you, when you pray, go into your inner room, close your door and pray to your Father who is in secret, and your Father who sees what is done in secret will reward you.*

7  *"And when you are praying, do not use meaningless repetition as the Gentiles do, for they suppose that they will be heard for their many words.*

8  *"So do not be like them; for your Father knows what you need before you ask Him.*

9  *"Pray, then, in this way:*

   *'Our Father who is in heaven,*

   *Hallowed be Your name.*

10 *'Your kingdom come.*

   *Your will be done,*

   *On earth as it is in heaven.*

11 *'Give us this day our daily bread.*

12 *'And forgive us our debts, as we also have forgiven our debtors.*

### ONE STEP FURTHER:

**Get the Whole Context**

If you have time this week, read the Sermon on the Mount in Matthew 5–7. This will give you the full context of our "worry" passage. In this famous teaching Jesus explains to a large crowd of followers what "the life of a disciple" is. Note below how Jesus' teaching compares with current cultural thinking.

NO WORRIES
Learning to Trust Our Sovereign God

*13 'And do not lead us into temptation, but deliver us from evil. [For Yours is the kingdom and the power and the glory forever. Amen.]'*

*14 "For if you forgive others for their transgressions, your heavenly Father will also forgive you.*

*15 "But if you do not forgive others, then your Father will not forgive your transgressions.*

**FYI:**

**Sea of Galilee Region**
Jesus delivered the Sermon on the Mount somewhere along the shore of the Sea of Galilee in northern Israel.

GALILEE

Sea of Galilee

Mediterranean Sea

Nazareth

SAMARIA

Jordan River

Jerusalem

JUDEA

Dead Sea

## DISCUSS with your group or PONDER on your own . . .

What does Jesus warn about in verse 1? What heart issue is He addressing? What payoff does this behavior have? What payoff does it miss?

What kinds of people does Jesus talk about in this section? List each group and describe what Jesus says about them.

What should people who practice righteousness be concerned about?

What are hypocrites concerned about? (If you've marked the word "men," go back and see what the text says.)

What kinds of worries do you face that are driven by a desire to please people?

What about those you influence? Do your friends or children struggle with worrying about what other people think? What kinds of worries do others bring to you?

Who should we seek to please? Why?

What behaviors does Jesus tell us to avoid?

What behaviors are assumed? What clues us into these?

What role does prayer play in your life today?

### I Thought *He* was the One with the Problem!

There was a time in my life not too many years ago when my husband and I were at a stand-off. Dave thought I had a problem with worry. I knew that he simply did not care enough . . . about anything. According to my life rubric at that time, if you didn't worry, you didn't care. I'll never forget the time he suggested that I "just stop" worrying about something.

Clearly the man was detached from reality. After all, I couldn't "just stop" worrying. Nobody could do *that*—at least not someone like me. He was asking me to stop being me. Worrying was hard-wired into my DNA. For my husband to suggest I "just stop" not only was crazy-talk, it was also a personal attack as far as I was concerned. It wasn't until God opened my eyes one day as I was reading Matthew 6 that I realized *I was the one with the problem*—and it was a sin problem.

Maybe you relate to this personally or maybe you know someone who lives with worry. Either way, I'm sure you've seen the damage worry brings to the lives of those it touches.

## NO WORRIES
Learning to Trust Our Sovereign God

## OBSERVE the TEXT of SCRIPTURE

As Jesus continues, He talks about fasting and treasures. We're going to focus more closely on this passage as it leads directly into "The Worry Text." "The Worry Text" (Matthew 6:25-34) starts off with the phrase "For this reason . . ." which means we need to find and pay close attention to what precedes it since it refers back to something in the text.

**READ** Matthew 6:16-24. **CIRCLE** every reference to *treasure*. (Use your concordance to find the verb forms of *treasure* that are hiding in the translation.) **UNDERLINE** every word that refers to eyes or seeing.

### Matthew 6:16-24

16  *"Whenever you fast, do not put on a gloomy face as the hypocrites do, for they neglect their appearance so that they will be noticed by men when they are fasting. Truly I say to you, they have their reward in full.*

17  *"But you, when you fast, anoint your head and wash your face*

18  *so that your fasting will not be noticed by men, but by your Father who is in secret; and your Father who sees what is done in secret will reward you.*

19  *"Do not store up for yourselves treasures on earth, where moth and rust destroy, and where thieves break in and steal.*

20  *"But store up for yourselves treasures in heaven, where neither moth nor rust destroys, and where thieves do not break in or steal;*

21  *for where your treasure is, there your heart will be also.*

22  *"The eye is the lamp of the body; so then if your eye is clear, your whole body will be full of light.*

23  *"But if your eye is bad, your whole body will be full of darkness. If then the light that is in you is darkness, how great is the darkness!*

24  *"No one can serve two masters; for either he will hate the one and love the other, or he will be devoted to one and despise the other. You cannot serve God and wealth.*

## DISCUSS with your group or PONDER on your own . . .

Briefly compare Jesus' words about fasting to his words about giving and praying.

What choice do people have in storing up treasures?

---

## INDUCTIVE TOOLS:

### Context is King

Context is king in matters of interpretation. We always need to pay attention to the neighborhoods where our texts live. That said, we need to pay even closer attention in a topical study where it can be tempting to overlook context when a single verse fits our biases while standing alone. No verses stand alone, all are connected to their environments.

### Don't Go There

Worry is a trap for many of us. We look at facts, put the worst spin on them and often end up "awfulizing." You know how that looks. It takes things to the ultimate.

Your child is stung by a bee and you immediately see her arm being removed because of a horrible infection you recently read about in a magazine. Now, chances are that she'll recover from her bee sting with little damage but the worry in you has caused an "awful" reaction in your mind.

You have "awfulized" and experienced all the pain of a real, tragic event. Your brain doesn't know the difference.

Why go there? Why borrow trouble? Why worry about something that hasn't happened? Think about it.

*Notes*

What endangers treasures stored up on earth?

What problems do earthly treasures bring? How can they affect the heart?

**ONE STEP FURTHER:**

**Word Study: Treasure**
If you have some extra time this week, find the Greek noun translated *treasure* as well as the corresponding verb that also appears in Matthew 6. Note how many times the root appears in Matthew 6:19-21 and record what you learn about it.

What is the benefit of storing treasures in heaven?

Why not hedge the risks by storing in both locations?

How is treasure related to the heart? Give one example of this truth in your life.

**NO WORRIES**
Learning to Trust Our Sovereign God

Week One: **The Sin We Excuse**

What does Jesus say about multiple masters?

**Worry and Women**

If we women were honest, I think most of us would say we're natural worriers because we're nurturers. We feel the responsibility and the anxiety of taking care of those we love. Whether they are under our care or out of our sight, it is hard not to worry. Health, finances, relationships, spiritual growth, futures, choices and consequences all give us great concern.

When it feels as if the world and all of its problems are on their shoulders, many women do the only thing they know to do, worry. In fact, in many cultures and social circles, "LOVE" is spelled "W-O-R-R-Y." If you don't worry, you don't love.

Concern about an issue is not worry. It's what you do with concern that makes the difference. I've found that when women find out that God is in the business of dealing with our cares, concerns and anxieties, things change. Life still happens but worry doesn't!

Do you ever worry about finances or physical items? If so, when and what?

Is this a "master" problem? Why/why not?

## OBSERVE the TEXT of SCRIPTURE

In Matthew 6:25-34, Jesus delivers a clear, repeated command.

**READ** Matthew 6:25-34. **CIRCLE** every reference to *worry*. Again, **UNDERLINE** every word that refers to eyes or seeing.

### *Matthew 6:25-34*

25 *"For this reason I say to you, do not be worried about your life,* as to *what you will eat or what you will drink; nor for your body,* as to *what you will put on. Is not life more than food, and the body more than clothing?*

26 *"Look at the birds of the air, that they do not sow, nor reap nor gather into barns, and yet your heavenly Father feeds them. Are you not worth much more than they?*

27 *"And who of you by being worried can add a single hour to his life?*

28 *"And why are you worried about clothing? Observe how the lilies of the field grow; they do not toil nor do they spin,*

29  *yet I say to you that not even Solomon in all his glory clothed himself like one of these.*

30  *"But if God so clothes the grass of the field, which is* alive *today and tomorrow is thrown into the furnace,* will He *not much more* clothe *you? You of little faith!*

31  *"Do not worry then, saying, 'What will we eat?' or 'What will we drink?' or 'What will we wear for clothing?'*

32  *"For the Gentiles eagerly seek all these things; for your heavenly Father knows that you need all these things.*

33  *"But seek first His kingdom and His righteousness, and all these things will be added to you.*

34  *"So do not worry about tomorrow; for tomorrow will care for itself. Each day has enough trouble of its own.*

## DISCUSS with your group or PONDER on your own . . .

Jesus begins verse 25 with the transition "For this reason" (Greek: *dia touto*, literally "because [of] this). What is He referring back to?

What common worries does Jesus identify?

Do you identify with any of these? If so, which ones?

How many times does He command His hearers not to worry?

### The Day My Ears Finally Heard

I can't tell you how many times I'd either read or heard Matthew 6 without realizing that Jesus was commanding, not suggesting. My personal sin deafened me to the command and blinded me to the solution. I breezed over Jesus' words "do not be worried" thinking they didn't apply to me since I was "a worrier." I thought, "You can't tell a worrier not to worry, right?" It's like telling an adulterer not to commit adultery, a thief not to steal. Hmmmm.

Jesus' *commands* His followers not to worry in Matthew 6:25 (imperative, plural) but He doesn't just command. He immediately tells us how to obey by providing empowering concrete examples. Instead of focusing on our worries, we're to look to our sovereign God who feeds birds and clothes lilies.

No Worries
Learning to Trust Our Sovereign God

What does He ask them about their worries?

## ONE STEP FURTHER:

### The Luke Connection
Luke records much of the same content in the account he compiles for Theophilus. If you have some extra time this week, compare Luke 12 with Matthew 6. Record your observations below.

What replacement behavior does He command?

What assurances does He give?

Is this easier said than done? Why/why not?

Did you answer the previous question remembering that Christians have the indwelling Holy Spirit? What difference does the indwelling Holy Spirit make in combatting worry? Explain.

# Digging Deeper

## Worriers in the Word: Torah

If you're up for a real challenge, each week you can take to the pages of Scripture to identify where worry situations show up in the lives of biblical characters and what outcomes they reaped either by giving in to worry or, conversely, by trusting God in spite of circumstances. We'll point you toward a number of accounts but it will be up to you to look for more. This week we'll limit our broad thinking to the pages of the Torah—Genesis, Exodus, Leviticus, Numbers, and Deuteronomy. One simple way to do this assignment is to listen to these broader portions of Scripture on an audio Bible and jot down notes as worriers cross your path.

What individuals and/or nations worried? How did they behave? What resulted?

What characters persevered in the midst of worrisome situations? How were they able to stand?

What is the most significant lesson you learned from the situations and outcomes you studied?

### Worry Causes Stress and Stress Can Kill You

Stress is a major issue in our culture. I hear people frequently say, "I'm stressed out," or "I've got to get rid of this stress." Have you ever said it? Have you ever thought it? If so, you are carrying around the burden of worry.

Worry is stress and the wrong kind of stress causes damage to your body. Your heart and intestines are particularly sensitive to toxic hormones your body produces when under stress. So, this whole subject of "worry" is a big deal, a bigger deal than many of us like to think. God in His kindness and great love has given us ways to handle worry. If we believe Him and really do what he says when worry tries to overtake us, then we will be able to manage the stress that it brings in it's wake.

God has pled with us and commanded us to stop the worrying and to rely on Him. It's good for us. It helps our spiritual and physical health and in so many ways, it allows us to speak well of Him to a world that is "worried sick."

## @THE END OF THE DAY . . .

Jesus commanded His followers not to worry; that means it's a sin we need to jettison. Although we often dismiss it as a minor character flaw that "doesn't hurt anyone," Jesus says "No!" to it. It not only makes the worrier miserable—which most worriers will attest to—it also exposes the worrier as a practical atheist behaving as though God either doesn't exist or does exist but is not in control. Before you call it a day, take some time to write down where practical atheism most often rears its ugly head in your life. If you need to confess the sin of worry to God or ask Him to help you walk in the reality of His sovereignty, take some time to do that, too.

# Week Two
## Choking the Word

*And the one on whom seed was sown among the thorns, this is the man who hears the word, and the worry of the world and the deceitfulness of wealth choke the word, and it becomes unfruitful.*
*–Matthew 13:22*

According to Hebrews 4:12 "the Word of God is living and active and sharper than any two-edged sword, and piercing as far as the division of soul and spirit, of both joints and marrow, and able to judge the thoughts and intentions of the heart." Paul refers to God's Word as "the sword of the Spirit." Throughout Psalm 119 the psalmist writes of the power of God's Word to comfort, transform, and empower those who follow God's Word and ways. Why is it, then, that so many sincere Bible-reading, Bible-believing people continue to flounder in the deep sea of worry? Why does this powerful Word seem powerless to so many?

This week we're going to look at a parable Jesus told about the Word and His chilling explanation about the effect our worry can have on the Word and consequently on us.

### The Power of God's Truth Over Our Fears

My mother was big on memorizing scripture, which was good because, as I've already told you, as a child I worried a lot. In my mind, there was a monster living at the top of the stairs. So, every night was a challenge. I hated going to bed because I just knew the monster would be waiting but then there was Mother. She taught me "What time I am afraid, I will put my trust in Thee." She repeated it over and over as she followed me up the stairs for a few harrowing nights. She was there but I still had to walk into the dark where the monster lived. It worried me every time bed time came around but Mother kept telling me, "What time I am afraid, I will put my trust in Thee."

Finally, one night I was on my own. She said, "You can do it!" I had to quit worrying about it and trust God because I was worried about what that monster was going to do. I still remember the rhythmical cadence of walking up the steps. "What--time--I am--afraid---I--will--put--my--trust--in--Thee." As I said it over and over, the fear (and therefore the worry) seemed to go away.

Even though I was very young, those beautiful, powerful words made the monster disappear. The power of the Word is greater than we can begin to imagine! You're never too young or too old to put that Word in your head. It pushes out the worry and calms your anxious heart.

## NO WORRIES
Learning to Trust Our Sovereign God

# WHAT WORRY DOES

This week we're going to look at a parable Jesus tells. It is recorded in each of the Synoptic Gospels—Matthew, Mark, and Luke. In each account we'll pay close attention to what Jesus says about the Word and worry.

## SETTING the SCENE

Jesus speaks parables to the crowd publicly and explanations to His disciples in private.

## OBSERVE the TEXT of SCRIPTURE

**READ** Matthew 13:1-23 and **CIRCLE** every reference to the *word*. You may need to read the parable twice to find the synonyms.

### Matthew 13:1-23

1  That day Jesus went out of the house and was sitting by the sea.

2  And large crowds gathered to Him, so He got into a boat and sat down, and the whole crowd was standing on the beach.

3  And He spoke many things to them in parables, saying, "Behold, the sower went out to sow;

4  and as he sowed, some seeds *fell beside the road*, and the birds came and ate them up.

5  "Others fell on the rocky places, where they did not have much soil; and immediately they sprang up, because they had no depth of soil.

6  "But when the sun had risen, they were scorched; and because they had no root, they withered away.

7  "Others fell among the thorns, and the thorns came up and choked them out.

8  "And others fell on the good soil and yielded a crop, some a hundredfold, some sixty, and some thirty.

9  "He who has ears, let him hear."

10  And the disciples came and said to Him, "Why do You speak to them in parables?"

11  Jesus answered them, "To you it has been granted to know the mysteries of the kingdom of heaven, but to them it has not been granted.

12 *"For whoever has, to him more shall be given, and he will have an abundance; but whoever does not have, even what he has shall be taken away from him.*

13 *"Therefore I speak to them in parables; because while seeing they do not see, and while hearing they do not hear, nor do they understand.*

14 *"In their case the prophecy of Isaiah is being fulfilled, which says,*

*'YOU WILL KEEP ON HEARING, BUT WILL NOT UNDERSTAND;*

*YOU WILL KEEP ON SEEING, BUT WILL NOT PERCEIVE;*

15 *FOR THE HEART OF THIS PEOPLE HAS BECOME DULL,*

*WITH THEIR EARS THEY SCARCELY HEAR,*

*AND THEY HAVE CLOSED THEIR EYES,*

*OTHERWISE THEY WOULD SEE WITH THEIR EYES,*

*HEAR WITH THEIR EARS,*

*AND UNDERSTAND WITH THEIR HEART AND RETURN,*

*AND I WOULD HEAL THEM.'*

16 *"But blessed are your eyes, because they see; and your ears, because they hear.*

17 *"For truly I say to you that many prophets and righteous men desired to see what you see, and did not see it, and to hear what you hear, and did not hear it.*

18 *"Hear then the parable of the sower.*

19 *"When anyone hears the word of the kingdom and does not understand it, the evil one comes and snatches away what has been sown in his heart. This is the one on whom seed was sown beside the road.*

20 *"The one on whom seed was sown on the rocky places, this is the man who hears the word and immediately receives it with joy;*

21 *yet he has no firm root in himself, but is only temporary, and when affliction or persecution arises because of the word, immediately he falls away.*

22 *"And the one on whom seed was sown among the thorns, this is the man who hears the word, and the worry of the world and the deceitfulness of wealth choke the word, and it becomes unfruitful.*

23 *"And the one on whom seed was sown on the good soil, this is the man who hears the word and understands it; who indeed bears fruit and brings forth, some a hundredfold, some sixty, and some thirty."*

---

**FYI:**

**Synoptic Gospels**

Matthew, Mark, and Luke are often referred to as the Synoptic Gospels. "Synoptic" literally means viewing or seeing together. Each of these Gospels accounts unfolds the events of Jesus' life in a similar fashion although they don't all include exactly the same events. The Gospel of John, while overlapping in some of its material, has more theological narrative in accord with John's stated purpose for writing: "Therefore many other signs Jesus also performed in the presence of the disciples, which are not written in this book; but these have been written so that you may believe that Jesus is the Christ, the Son of God; and that believing you may have life in His name" (John 20:30-31). The specific signs John chooses to record are:

1. Turning water to wine (John 2),

2. Healing an official's son (John 4),

3. Healing a paralytic at the pool of Bethesda (John 5),

4. Feeding 5,000 (John 6),

5. Walking on water (John 6),

6. Restoring sight to the blind (John 9), and

7. Raising Lazarus from the dead (John 11).

**FYI:**

**Reading Tip: Begin with prayer**

You may have heard this a million times over and if this is a million and one, so be it. Whenever you read or study God's Word, first pray and ask His Spirit to be your Guide.

**NO WORRIES**
Learning to Trust Our Sovereign God

## DISCUSS with your group or PONDER on your own . . .

According to Matthew 13:3-9, where does the sower sow seed? Describe the different soils.

What happens to the seed in each of the soils?

How much does the seed on good soil yield? Are harvests the same? If not, how do they differ?

Jesus explains the parable to His disciples in verses 19-23. How does He further describe *the word* in verse 19? What is this "word"?

How does the seed sown on the rocky soil start out?

What happens to it when affliction or persecution arises because of the word? What is lacking?

# Digging Deeper

## Worriers in the Word: The Period of Joshua and the Judges

This week as we consider worrisome situations in the pages of Scripture, we'll focus our attention on the time frame of Joshua and the judges of Israel. This frame stretches across the biblical texts of Joshua, Judges, Ruth and the beginning chapters of 1 Samuel. Remember, we're surveying the biblical text for worriers, non-worriers, and how the two responses to worrisome situations turned out for their owners.

How does Rahab's thinking compare with the thinking of her countrymen according to Joshua 2? What results come from each?

What were some other responses to worrisome situations? If some stood up against opposition, how did they do it?

Who crumbled in the face of hard circumstances?

Compare the thinking of the worriers and the non-worriers. What differences did you notice? What can you learn from their lives and the results of their thinking and subsequent behavior?

ONE STEP FURTHER:

**Fruit**
If you have some extra time this week, read John 15 taking careful note of what Jesus says about fruit. Record your observations below.

NO WORRIES
Learning to Trust Our Sovereign God

How do you respond to affliction? Are you aware that God has purposes for it in the lives of believers? (Hold that thought. More on Romans 5 later.)

Have you ever experienced persecution? If so, briefly describe your experience. Did you know that persecution is part of the future of "those who desire to live godly in Christ Jesus"?

Sometimes we worry that we will face affliction or persecution. The Bible tells us that if we follow Jesus we will face them both. The question is not how to avoid them (we can't!) but rather how to respond when they inevitably come our way. As we'll see later in our study, God uses affliction to build character.

How does Jesus explain the seed sown among the thorns? What chokes the word?

Compare Jesus' connection of worry and wealth in Matthew 13 with His connection of worry and treasure in Matthew 6 and record your observations.

**JAN SNAPSHOT**

**Blinding and Deafening**

Do you ever think about how worry can keep you from embracing what God has already given you?

I talked with two people who were concerned about their marriage. We couldn't make much headway, though, because each of them was so worried about what the other might do. (I'd call that lack of trust but that makes us worry, too!) Their worry blocked their ability to embrace what was happening in their marriage and see that there might be a way to repair some of their issues.

They both had reasons to feel fearful about the future because of things that had happened in the past, but God was changing them. Still they couldn't see it because they were WORRIED! All they had to do was stop worrying to see that God had cleared the path ahead of them if they would just dare to trust Him and each other!

Worry often blinds and deafens us to the good things God is doing for us because we are so afraid someone's going to trump His goodness and "get us." Laying down the worry makes God look so much bigger and the reality is He is even bigger than what you think!

**FYI:**

**How many?**

*"Indeed, all who desire to live godly in Christ Jesus will be persecuted."*

–2 Timothy 3:12

*Notes*

How does the person described by the good soil differ from the others?

Is an unfruitful "Christian" a Christian? Explain your answer from Scripture.

## OBSERVE the TEXT of SCRIPTURE

This time we'll look at Mark's record of Jesus' parable of the sower.

**READ** Mark 4:1-20. Again, **CIRCLE** every reference to *word* including synonyms and pronouns.

### Mark 4:1-20

1  *He began to teach again by the sea. And such a very large crowd gathered to Him that He got into a boat in the sea and sat down; and the whole crowd was by the sea on the land.*

2  *And He was teaching them many things in parables, and was saying to them in His teaching,*

3  *"Listen to this! Behold, the sower went out to sow;*

4  *as he was sowing, some seed fell beside the road, and the birds came and ate it up.*

5  *"Other seed fell on the rocky ground where it did not have much soil; and immediately it sprang up because it had no depth of soil.*

6  *"And after the sun had risen, it was scorched; and because it had no root, it withered away.*

7  *"Other seed fell among the thorns, and the thorns came up and choked it, and it yielded no crop.*

8  *"Other seeds fell into the good soil, and as they grew up and increased, they yielded a crop and produced thirty, sixty, and a hundredfold."*

9  *And He was saying, "He who has ears to hear, let him hear."*

No Worries
Learning to Trust Our Sovereign God

10  As soon as He was alone, His followers, along with the twelve, began *asking* Him about *the parables.*

11  And He was saying to them, "To you has been given the mystery of the kingdom of God, but those who are outside get everything in parables,

12  so that WHILE SEEING, THEY MAY SEE AND NOT PERCEIVE, AND WHILE HEARING, THEY MAY HEAR AND NOT UNDERSTAND, OTHERWISE THEY MIGHT RETURN AND BE FORGIVEN."

13  And He said to them, "Do you not understand this parable? How will you understand all the parables?

14  "The sower sows the word.

15  "These are the ones who are beside the road where the word is sown; and when they hear, immediately Satan comes and takes away the word which has been sown in them.

16  "In a similar way these are the ones on whom seed was sown on the rocky places, *who*, when they hear the word, immediately receive it with joy;

17  and they have no firm *root* in themselves, but are only *temporary*; then, when affliction or persecution arises because of the word, immediately they fall away.

18  "And others are the ones on whom seed was sown among the thorns; these are the ones who have heard the word,

19  but the worries of the world, and the deceitfulness of riches, and the desires for other things enter in and choke the word, and it becomes unfruitful.

20  "And those are the ones on whom seed was sown on the good soil; and they hear the word and accept it and bear fruit, thirty, sixty, and a hundredfold."


## DISCUSS with your group or PONDER on your own . . .

Does receiving the word with joy evidence true conversion? Explain your answer from the text.

*Notes*

How does Mark's account of the seed sown among thorns compare with Matthew's? What does he mention that Matthew leaves out?

Again, according to Mark 4:19, what do these thorns do to the word and what is the result?

If worry can choke the word, how serious is it?

## OBSERVE the TEXT of SCRIPTURE

**READ** Luke 8:4-15. Again, **CIRCLE** every reference to *word* including synonyms and pronouns.

### *Luke 8:4-15*

4  *When a large crowd was coming together, and those from the various cities were journeying to Him, He spoke by way of a parable:*

5  *"The sower went out to sow his seed; and as he sowed, some fell beside the road, and it was trampled under foot and the birds of the air ate it up.*

6  *"Other seed fell on rocky soil, and as soon as it grew up, it withered away, because it had no moisture.*

7  *"Other seed fell among the thorns; and the thorns grew up with it and choked it out.*

NO WORRIES
Learning to Trust Our Sovereign God

8 *"Other* seed *fell into the good soil, and grew up, and produced a crop a hundred times as great." As He said these things, He would call out, "He who has ears to hear, let him hear."*

9 *His disciples* began *questioning Him as to what this parable meant.*

10 *And He said, "To you it has been granted to know the mysteries of the kingdom of God, but to the rest* it is *in parables, so that SEEING THEY MAY NOT SEE, AND HEARING THEY MAY NOT UNDERSTAND.*

11 *"Now the parable is this: the seed is the word of God.*

12 *"Those beside the road are those who have heard; then the devil comes and takes away the word from their heart, so that they will not believe and be saved.*

13 *"Those on the rocky* soil are *those who, when they hear, receive the word with joy; and these have no* firm *root; they believe for a while, and in time of temptation fall away.*

14 *"The* seed *which fell among the thorns, these are the ones who have heard, and as they go on their way they are choked with worries and riches and pleasures of* this *life, and bring no fruit to maturity.*

15 *"But the seed* in the good soil, *these are the ones who have heard the word in an honest and good heart, and hold it fast, and bear fruit with perseverance.*

### DISCUSS with your group or PONDER on your own . . .

Do the disciples understand the parable immediately? How are they finally able to understand it?

According to Luke 8:11, what is the seed?

*Notes*

Describe the conditions that cause the seed on the rocky soil to fail.

What chokes the seed among the thorns according to Luke 8:14? How do the details in this account compare with those in the other accounts?

**FYI:**

**Using a Concordance**
A great way to find appropriate cross-references is to search on a key word in a text in its original language. Finding out how a key word is used elsewhere in Scripture is very beneficial!

If you need help, check out the Resources section for step-by-step instructions on using an online concordance.

Compare the outcomes of the seed among the thorns and the seed that fell on the good soil.

Which plant bears fruit? What is involved in bearing fruit?

NO WORRIES
Learning to Trust Our Sovereign God

# Digging Deeper

## Soils Two and Three

If you have some extra time this week, dig a little more into soils two and three and see what light other Scripture sheds on them. Search for appropriate cross-references. Here are a few to get you started: Romans 5, James 1, 2 Corinthians, 1 Peter 1.

| Soil Two Challenges | What it Causes | What Other Scriptures Say |
| --- | --- | --- |
| affliction [*thlipsis*] (Matt 13:21, Mark 4:7) | | |

| Soil Three Challenges | What it Causes | What Other Scriptures Say |
| --- | --- | --- |

Summarize your findings below.

# WHAT TRIBULATION DOES

Most people fear trials and tribulations, real *and* imagined. But God's Word tells us tribulation has purpose. Let's take a look at this worry-combatting truth.

## OBSERVE the TEXT of SCRIPTURE

**READ** Romans 5:1–11. **CIRCLE** every reference to *tribulation.* Then, **UNDERLINE** the cascading qualities that result from it.

### *Romans 5:1-11*

1  *Therefore, having been justified by faith, we have peace with God through our Lord Jesus Christ,*

2  *through whom also we have obtained our introduction by faith into this grace in which we stand; and we exult in hope of the glory of God.*

3  *And not only this, but we also exult in our tribulations, knowing that tribulation brings about perseverance;*

4  *and perseverance, proven character; and proven character, hope;*

5  *and hope does not disappoint, because the love of God has been poured out within our hearts through the Holy Spirit who was given to us.*

6  *For while we were still helpless, at the right time Christ died for the ungodly.*

7  *For one will hardly die for a righteous man; though perhaps for the good man someone would dare even to die.*

8  *But God demonstrates His own love toward us, in that while we were yet sinners, Christ died for us.*

9  *Much more then, having now been justified by His blood, we shall be saved from the wrath of God through Him.*

10  *For if while we were enemies we were reconciled to God through the death of His Son, much more, having been reconciled, we shall be saved by His life.*

11  *And not only this, but we also exult in God through our Lord Jesus Christ, through whom we have now received the reconciliation.*

### JAN SNAPSHOT

**Woulda, Shoulda**

Worry almost draws a picture in the way it is spelled. The word itself looks like the word, *"wormy."*

When I think of something being wormy, I think of rolling back rocks and seeing squirming creatures making inroads in the dirt. Worry is like this. It squirms into our thoughts and makes little inroads we don't know are there. Until we stop and look at why we are anxious, we may never know that the worms of worry have taken over— we may never know that our thoughts have become "wormy."

Wormy thoughts are riddled with, "What if?"s, "I should have!"s, and "If only"s. Wormy thoughts keep us focused on ourselves and what may or may not happen to us.

I can recognize my wormy thoughts by the anxiety I experience. When I begin to feel that old familiar discomfort, I stop and think, "What has me worried?" If I think long enough, I usually can go back to the moment the first thought hit me that started the cascade of worries. Then, I identify it, challenge it, and replace it. That's how I exterminate the "wormies." It's a job to pin-point sometimes but if you are intentional, you can do it. Like turning up rocks to find worms, if you are intentional, you'll find them!

## DISCUSS with your group or PONDER on your own . . .

What ultimate stable foundation does our life rest on according to Romans 5:1?

**FYI:**

**Exulting**
Exulting or boasting in our tribulations includes a sense of rejoicing in them knowing that God is doing a work in our lives through them.

What does Paul tell his readers to exult in? Why?

What will tribulation eventually bring about in a true follower of Jesus?

How can this truth help you stand firm in times of tribulation?

Are you living in the light of this truth today?

*Notes*

## @THE END OF THE DAY . . .

One of the reasons worry is such a big deal is that Jesus tells us it can choke the Word. Yet, ironically, this Word is our strongest weapon against worry and every other sin we face. In the Word we learn that as believers we can rest, trust and live at peace because we serve a sovereign God who loves us, who has saved us, and who is good. We'll look at the bedrock truth of God's sovereignty next week.

NO WORRIES
Learning to Trust Our Sovereign God

# It Only Works if God is Sovereign

*You are good and do good; teach me Your statutes.*
–Psalm 119:68

Part of breaking "the anxieties of this age" (Mark 4:19) is realizing that they are not our friends; they don't keep us safe. This worry doesn't keep our children alive. It doesn't make us smarter than everyone else. It is a tool our adversary uses to choke the Word. We are safe only in the arms of our sovereign God where nothing can reach us that He does not allow. God does save us from some dangers in this life, but temporal safety by its very definition is not ultimately safe because it ends. It is ephemeral, fading away like the wind. God's safety is eternal. His power, love, and goodness know no limits. As the psalmist says, "You are good and do good."

This week we'll begin to look for ourselves at what the Bible says about God, what He does, and how these truths impact the way we think and act.

## SETTING the SCENE

We overviewed Matthew 6 in Week One, looking specifically at Jesus' repeated "Don't worry" command and His picture of God's lavish provision for much lesser valued (two for a penny) creatures. This week we'll look more closely at what the passage teaches about God.

## OBSERVE the TEXT of SCRIPTURE

**REVIEW** Matthew 6:25–34. This time **CIRCLE** every reference to *God* including synonyms.

### Matthew 6:25-34

25  *"For this reason I say to you, do not be worried about your life, as to what you will eat or what you will drink; nor for your body, as to what you will put on. Is not life more than food, and the body more than clothing?*

26  *"Look at the birds of the air, that they do not sow, nor reap nor gather into barns, and yet your heavenly Father feeds them. Are you not worth much more than they?*

27  *"And who of you by being worried can add a single hour to his life?*

28  *"And why are you worried about clothing? Observe how the lilies of the field grow; they do not toil nor do they spin,*

29  *yet I say to you that not even Solomon in all his glory clothed himself like one of these.*

30  *"But if God so clothes the grass of the field, which is alive today and tomorrow is thrown into the furnace, will He not much more clothe you? You of little faith!*

31  *"Do not worry then, saying, 'What will we eat?' or 'What will we drink?' or 'What will we wear for clothing?'*

32  *"For the Gentiles eagerly seek all these things; for your heavenly Father knows that you need all these things.*

33  *"But seek first His kingdom and His righteousness, and all these things will be added to you.*

34  *"So do not worry about tomorrow; for tomorrow will care for itself. Each day has enough trouble of its own.*

---

**FYI:**

**Tomorrow**

In verse 34 we see another from the worry word group, translated "care" *(merimnao)*. Matthew 6:34 literally reads "So do not worry about tomorrow; for tomorrow will worry for itself."

---

NO WORRIES
Learning to Trust Our Sovereign God

## DISCUSS with your group or PONDER on your own . . .

What three-word phrase does Jesus use to describe God in this section and throughout Matthew 5–7?

Why should this make it easier for us to trust Him?

How does God change our false opinions of Him? What does He do?

What does God do according to this text? Look for the verbs to help you answer.

What are your needs today? Does God know your needs, too?

**FYI:**

**Your Heavenly Father**
There is a world of difference between a beloved father and an impersonal power.

**ONE STEP FURTHER:**

**Word Studies: Eagerly Seek and Seek**
If you have some extra time this week, see if you can find the Greek words translated *eagerly seek* and *seek*. Do they mean the same thing or something different? Where else are they used in the Word? How are they used? Record your findings below.

**No Worries**
Learning to Trust Our Sovereign God

# GOD IS BIGGER THAN OUR WORRY . . .

. . . and everything else for that matter.

The Word of God is the way we come to know our sovereign and trustworthy God. It is critical that we look to Him and His Word in order to break the chains of worry.

Matthew 6 tells us specifically that God feeds, clothes, knows the future, and adds to life. We'll consider each of these categories, but first let's look at other passages in Scripture that give us additional information about the sovereignty of God Almighty!

### SETTING the SCENE

Let's start at the very beginning.

### OBSERVE the TEXT of SCRIPTURE

**READ** Genesis 1–2:7. **CIRCLE** every occurrence of *God* and **UNDERLINE** every verb describing His actions.

#### *Genesis 1–2:7*

1  *In the beginning God created the heavens and the earth.*

2  *The earth was formless and void, and darkness was over the surface of the deep, and the Spirit of God was moving over the surface of the waters.*

3  *Then God said, "Let there be light"; and there was light.*

4  *God saw that the light was good; and God separated the light from the darkness.*

5  *God called the light day, and the darkness He called night. And there was evening and there was morning, one day.*

6  *Then God said, "Let there be an expanse in the midst of the waters, and let it separate the waters from the waters."*

7  *God made the expanse, and separated the waters which were below the expanse from the waters which were above the expanse; and it was so.*

8  *God called the expanse heaven. And there was evening and there was morning, a second day.*

9  *Then God said, "Let the waters below the heavens be gathered into one place, and let the dry land appear"; and it was so.*

10  *God called the dry land earth, and the gathering of the waters He called seas; and God saw that it was good.*

11  *Then God said, "Let the earth sprout vegetation, plants yielding seed, and fruit trees on the earth bearing fruit after their kind with seed in them"; and it was so.*

---

12 *The earth brought forth vegetation, plants yielding seed after their kind, and trees bearing fruit with seed in them, after their kind; and God saw that it was good.*

13 *There was evening and there was morning, a third day.*

14 *Then God said, "Let there be lights in the expanse of the heavens to separate the day from the night, and let them be for signs and for seasons and for days and years;*

15 *and let them be for lights in the expanse of the heavens to give light on the earth"; and it was so.*

16 *God made the two great lights, the greater light to govern the day, and the lesser light to govern the night; He made the stars also.*

17 *God placed them in the expanse of the heavens to give light on the earth,*

18 *and to govern the day and the night, and to separate the light from the darkness; and God saw that it was good.*

19 *There was evening and there was morning, a fourth day.*

20 *Then God said, "Let the waters teem with swarms of living creatures, and let birds fly above the earth in the open expanse of the heavens."*

21 *God created the great sea monsters and every living creature that moves, with which the waters swarmed after their kind, and every winged bird after its kind; and God saw that it was good.*

22 *God blessed them, saying, "Be fruitful and multiply, and fill the waters in the seas, and let birds multiply on the earth."*

23 *There was evening and there was morning, a fifth day.*

24 *Then God said, "Let the earth bring forth living creatures after their kind: cattle and creeping things and beasts of the earth after their kind"; and it was so.*

25 *God made the beasts of the earth after their kind, and the cattle after their kind, and everything that creeps on the ground after its kind; and God saw that it was good.*

26 *Then God said, "Let Us make man in Our image, according to Our likeness; and let them rule over the fish of the sea and over the birds of the sky and over the cattle and over all the earth, and over every creeping thing that creeps on the earth."*

27 *God created man in His own image, in the image of God He created him; male and female He created them.*

28 *God blessed them; and God said to them, "Be fruitful and multiply, and fill the earth, and subdue it; and rule over the fish of the sea and over the birds of the sky and over every living thing that moves on the earth."*

29 *Then God said, "Behold, I have given you every plant yielding seed that is on the surface of all the earth, and every tree which has fruit yielding seed; it shall be food for you;*

NO WORRIES
Learning to Trust Our Sovereign God

*30* *and to every beast of the earth and to every bird of the sky and to every thing that moves on the earth which has life, I have given* every green plant for food*"; and it was so.*

*31* *God saw all that He had made, and behold, it was very good. And there was evening and there was morning, the sixth day.*

### Genesis 2

*1* *Thus the heavens and the earth were completed, and all their hosts.*

*2* *By the seventh day God completed His work which He had done, and He rested on the seventh day from all His work which He had done.*

*3* *Then God blessed the seventh day and sanctified it, because in it He rested from all His work which God had created and made.*

*4* *This is the account of the heavens and the earth when they were created, in the day that the LORD God made earth and heaven.*

*5* *Now no shrub of the field was yet in the earth, and no plant of the field had yet sprouted, for the LORD God had not sent rain upon the earth, and there was no man to cultivate the ground.*

*6* *But a mist used to rise from the earth and water the whole surface of the ground.*

*7* *Then the LORD God formed man of dust from the ground, and breathed into his nostrils the breath of life; and man became a living being.*

## DISCUSS with your group or PONDER on your own . . .

What did you learn about God in this section?

What did God do? If you're a list maker, now's a good time to make one. Use the verbs you underlined to "bullet" your list.

Did anything come into being apart from God?

What do you see in common with Matthew 6? What does God provide according to both passages?

Where does human life come from?

According to this passage, how powerful is God? Is this enough power to trust in, to put your worries to rest? Why/why not?

Week Three: **It Only Works if God is Sovereign**

## SETTING the SCENE

In the following Christological passage, we see Who holds creation together. The context tells us that the "He" in the passage is Jesus.

---

**ONE STEP FURTHER:**

**Word Study: Hold Together**
If you have some time this week, find the Greek word translated *hold together*. What does the statement "in Him all things hold together" teach us? See what you can learn about it and record your findings below.

## OBSERVE the TEXT of SCRIPTURE

**READ** Colossians 1:15-17. **CIRCLE** every description and pronoun referring to Jesus. **UNDERLINE** every occurrence of the phrase *all things*.

### Colossians 1:15–17

15  He [Jesus] is the image of the invisible God, the firstborn of all creation.

16  For by Him all things were created, both *in the heavens and on earth, visible and invisible, whether thrones or dominions or rulers or authorities*—all things have been created through Him and for Him.

17  He is before all things, and in Him all things hold together.

## DISCUSS with your group or PONDER on your own . . .

What does the passage teach about Jesus?

Specifically, what was His role in the creation of the world?

Does anything exist before Him? Explain.

What is His role in the universe now?

Is there anything that He is not prior to, has not created, or does not sustain?

Does the text leave room for anything beyond His control?

What assurance does this give to people in relationship with Him?

### Filtered through Fingers of Love

As a Christian living in the last quarter of life, I look back with amazement at just how in control our God has been.

That is one of the sweetest truths I learned when I first began to study the Bible under Kay Arthur. Before I knew her as a friend, I knew her as a teacher and will ever be grateful that she taught me that nothing touches me that is not first "filtered through His fingers of love." That was life-changing.

I, who worried about so much, began to see that the God I was learning to know was sovereign. That meant He reigns. He rules. He has everything in His Hand and because of that I am safe. I'm not safe from trials and tribulations. They are part of life. I am, however, safe in His Hands.

He is sovereign over my life, your life, our children and our children's children and all that could concern you or me. There is nothing we can do to remove ourselves from His keeping, so why would we worry? Why would we fret? If we stumble or are knocked down, we're still in His Hand. It is so big, it covers all things that happen in this world and holds on to us at the same time. Put that in your brain and roll it around!

## SETTING the SCENE

God not only creates and sustains, He kills and makes alive. Deuteronomy 32, the Song of Moses, records Moses' words to the Israelites just prior to his death and their entry into the Promised Land. In verse 39 God speaks directly to them through Moses.

## OBSERVE the TEXT of SCRIPTURE

**READ** Deuteronomy 32:39. **CIRCLE** references to *God* and **UNDERLINE** everything God does.

### *Deuteronomy 32:39*

39   *'See now that I, I am He,*

     *And there is no god besides Me;*

     *It is I who put to death and give life.*

     *I have wounded and it is I who heal,*

     *And there is no one who can deliver from My hand.*

## DISCUSS with your group or PONDER on your own . . .

What specific actions does God do?

Does the text concern or comfort you? Think this through carefully and then defend your answer.

---

**ONE STEP FURTHER:**

**Deuteronomy 32**
Read the entire Song of Moses for the context. Record your observations on the text below.

NO WORRIES
Learning to Trust Our Sovereign God

40

# Digging Deeper

## Worriers in the Word: The United Kingdom of Israel

Israel was united during the reigns of Saul, David, and Solomon. Saul first appears on the biblical scene in 1 Samuel 9 and Israel stays united through 1 Kings 11. For more on David's life and times, be sure to check out the many Psalms he penned. Solomon wrote most of the book of Proverbs and probably wrote the Song of Solomon and Ecclesiastes, as well.

Compare these first three kings with one another and describe how they handled themselves in difficult and worrisome situations. Where did they turn? Who did they trust? How did they behave? How did their situations turn out? How did each view God and what kind of relationship did each have with Him?

Saul

David

Solomon

### When I Really Learned Sovereignty

If you had asked me in my early twenties whether or not I believed that God is sovereign, I'd have answered "Yes! Absolutely." My worry and behavior, however, denied my words.

While I said "God is sovereign," I lived my life like I was responsible for keeping everyone I cared about alive. That all changed when my daughter showed signs of kidney problems when she was two years old. She's fine now thanks to God's healing work through the hands of medical professionals, but after a roller-coaster ride that began with seizures and an ambulance and then years of dealing with medical testing for a chronic condition that could rear up at any time, I finally began to realize that I couldn't keep Katie alive. God was God in our health and in our sickness. I finally had to release the phantom hold that I had over her life to the hand of the Almighty God who already had everything under control.

I'll never forget coming to the realization that either God is sovereign or He's not and if He is (and I believe that with everything I've got!) then I can rest.

## SETTING the SCENE

Daniel 4 takes us forward in the history of God's people to a time when the empire of Babylon under the leadership of King Nebuchadnezzar held the people of Judah in captivity for 70 years. The following text recounts the experience and words of Nebuchadnezzar, King of Babylon and most of the known world at the time.

## OBSERVE the TEXT of SCRIPTURE

**READ** Daniel 4:28-37 and **BOX** every reference to *Nebuchadnezzar* including pronouns. **CIRCLE** every reference to *the Most High* including pronouns and synonyms.

*Daniel 4:28-37*

28  "All this happened to Nebuchadnezzar the king.

29  "Twelve months later he was walking on the roof of the royal palace of Babylon.

30  "The king reflected and said, 'Is this not Babylon the great, which I myself have built as a royal residence by the might of my power and for the glory of my majesty?'

31  "While the word was in the king's mouth, a voice came from heaven, saying, 'King Nebuchadnezzar, to you it is declared: sovereignty has been removed from you,

32  and you will be driven away from mankind, and your dwelling place will be with the beasts of the field. You will be given grass to eat like cattle, and seven periods of time will pass over you until you recognize that the Most High is ruler over the realm of mankind and bestows it on whomever He wishes.'

33  "Immediately the word concerning Nebuchadnezzar was fulfilled; and he was driven away from mankind and began eating grass like cattle, and his body was drenched with the dew of heaven until his hair had grown like eagles' feathers and his nails like birds' claws.

34  "But at the end of that period, I, Nebuchadnezzar, raised my eyes toward heaven and my reason returned to me, and I blessed the Most High and praised and honored Him who lives forever;

For His dominion is an everlasting dominion,

And His kingdom endures from generation to generation.

35  "All the inhabitants of the earth are accounted as nothing,

But He does according to His will in the host of heaven

And among the inhabitants of earth;

And no one can ward off His hand

Or say to Him, 'What have You done?'

36  "At that time my reason returned to me. And my majesty and splendor were restored to me for the glory of my kingdom, and my counselors and my nobles began seeking me out; so I was reestablished in my sovereignty, and surpassing greatness was added to me.

*37* *"Now I, Nebuchadnezzar, praise, exalt and honor the King of heaven, for all His works are true and His ways just, and He is able to humble those who walk in pride."*

## DISCUSS with your group or PONDER on your own . . .

Describe Nebuchadnezzar. Who is he? What happens to him?

What does he learn about God? How does he learn it?

How does his thinking change?

Have you ever had a "Nebuchadnezzar moment" when you realized that God is sovereign over all? If so, how did it change you?

**FYI:**

**No Authority Except From God**

If you have some extra time this week, see what each of the follow passages say about human authority and record what you discover.

John 19:10–12

Romans 13:1–8

# Digging Deeper

## Who has the power of death?

God kills and makes alive . . . we're told this specifically and we see it played out over and over again. Yet what do we make of Hebrews 2:14–15 which reads "Therefore, since the children share in flesh and blood, He Himself likewise also partook of the same, that through death He might render powerless him who had the power of death, that is, the devil, and might free those who through fear of death were subject to slavery all their lives"? If you have some extra time and energy this week, dig into this question keeping in mind the clear teaching of Scripture we have already seen.

As you start off, consider where death originated and why it exists. Make sure to cite your references.

In what way does the devil hold the power of death? Again, answer from Scripture citing your references.

What power did Satan have over Job? How did he get it? Who limited it and in what ways? Explain.

What power did Satan have in Peter's life? How did he get it? How was it limited? Explain?

Why can Christians today live free from the fear of death?

## @THE END OF THE DAY . . .

Next week we'll look more at the sovereignty of God over all things and at His power in the affairs of men as we consider how this truth provides a firm foundation for our battle against worry. For now, though, take some time to reflect on the scriptures we studied this week. What truth did you most need to hear? Jot it down below along with how you'll be applying it in your life.

Maybe you've been fighting against a truth. Jot this down, too, and ask God to help you see and apply it as you pursue Him through His Word.

Remember, we'll fight many battles in our war on worry, but our God who fights for us will help us to stand. Progress measured over years is still progress.

# Sovereign Over Everything

> *"And which of you by worrying can add a single hour to his life's span? If then you cannot do even a very little thing, why do you worry about other matters?"*
> — Jesus (Luke 12:25–26)

Last week we saw that God created out of nothing, that in Jesus everything holds together, that God puts to death and gives life, wounds and heals. He raises up rulers and brings them down. This week we'll continue to look at His power beginning with a prophecy in the book of Isaiah and then considering specific categories Matthew talks about—feeding, clothing, knowing all things, and adding to life. As we study, remember that these are not dry facts about a distant power. We're studying about the Creator of the universe who has reached out to redeem us. If we are in Christ, God is our Father. And as Paul says in Romans 8:31 "If God is for us, who can be against us?" (ESV).

## ONE STEP FURTHER:

**The Sovereign God Who Seeks Us**

God is sovereign and involved. He seeks the lost. For a simple summary of man's predicament and God's intervention, check out these verses and record what you learn.

Romans 3:23

Romans 6:23

Romans 5:8

Ephesians 2:8–9

# GOD IS OVER AUTHORITIES

Today we're going to begin in a text from the prophetic book of Isaiah. Isaiah 44 and 45 show us God's foreknowledge, His sovereignty in raising up rulers, and His saving purpose among other things. Because we're picking up in the middle of something much bigger, it's important to make sure we read ample context. For this reason, please read the text in your Bible and then answer the questions below.

## SETTING the SCENE

Isaiah prophesies to people of Israel. Among other things, he predicts the rise of a ruler named Cyrus over 150 years in advance.

## OBSERVE the TEXT of SCRIPTURE

**READ** Isaiah 44–45 in your Bible paying close attention to everything God says about Himself.

## DISCUSS with your group or PONDER on your own . . .

How does God describe Himself in Isaiah 44:1-8?

What is a proper response to this?

---

## FYI:

**If God is for us, who is against us?**

*For those whom He foreknew, He also predestined to become conformed to the image of His Son, so that He would be the firstborn among many brethren; and these whom He predestined, He also called; and these whom He called, He also justified; and these whom He justified, He also glorified. What then shall we say to these things? If God is for us, who is against us? He who did not spare His own Son, but delivered Him over for us all, how will He not also with Him freely give us all things?*

—Romans 8:29-32

---

Describe what God says about the people's idolatry in Isaiah 44:9-20. How do they view their idols? What do they expect from them?

What do we worship in similar ways today? In what forbidden places do we look for deliverance?

Have you ever "held a lie in your right hand" (v. 20)? If so, how did it affect your thinking and subsequent behavior? What can break the power of a lie?

What does God say about His relationship to Israel in Isaiah 44:21-28?

### What Might Have Been?

"What might have been does not exist, so don't even go there." That's one of my favorite quotes. Yes, it's my quote that I believe God dropped in my head when I was thinking about all the things we wish we could control but can't. When we do dare to go to the "what might have beens" that we wish we had done differently or influenced differently, we are digging around looking for ways we could have controlled the non-existent or at the most, the uncontrollable.

We can make control look like something reputable. We make it sound (at least to ourselves) like something that will serve us well but look for its power in your life and how it affects your thinking and emotions.

1. How do you feel when events don't work out the way you want?

2. How do you feel when you can't fix something or someone who is broken?

3. How do you feel when someone you love follows a path that differs from the one you hoped they'd take?

If you're troubled by what you "could have, should have, would have done" then you're in the grip of worry. You're living in a fantasy land and the best thing you can do is to tell yourself, "What might have been does not exist, so don't even go there." Then repent! You'll be amazed how your worries will be diminished as your unholy need to control fades away!

## NO WORRIES
Learning to Trust Our Sovereign God

What kind of worries do you have that are tied with past transgressions? Have you accepted God's forgiveness?

What else do we learn about God in this section?

What does the text tell us about Cyrus?

How often does the word group *save (saved, salvation, Savior, etc.)* appear in Isaiah 45? What is the clear message? Who saves? Who can be saved?

# Digging Deeper

## He Feeds and Clothes

In Matthew 6 we see that God feeds and clothes, He knows and He adds to life. We'll look at His omniscience and power to add to life as we go over our main section texts. On your own this week, take some time to remember and consider the ways God cares for physical needs such as food and clothing.

What are some ways God provided food for His people throughout biblical history? (Think about the wilderness and the circumstances of some of the prophets to get you going.)

How did God provide for the needs of Levites, widows, orphans, and foreigners living within Israel?

How did God provide for some of the clothing needs of His people? (This is tougher, think broadly.)

How did God provide for other daily needs of people in the Bible?

*And my God will supply all your needs according to His riches in glory in Christ Jesus.*

—Philippians 4:19

**FYI:**

### Tips for Digging

Of course the most thorough way to dig deeper on questions that cover the breadth of Scripture is to read the whole Bible. Those who have done this one or more times will have a much easier time with subjects the entire Bible discusses.

So where does this leave others who haven't studied the whole Bible? Well, it certainly doesn't leave them out of the hunt, it just means that they'll use a little different approach until they have more biblical background.

One way to zero in on relevant texts is to search on key words or concepts in a concordance. For "food" you can search on *food*, *bread*, *manna*, etc., for "clothing" *clothing*, *sandals*, etc.

As you search via concordance and read the contexts of the verses you find, you'll continue to build a working knowledge of God's Word. Hopefully you'll be more and more drawn to reading the whole Book for yourself time and time again! Then, the overview questions will be a snap!

No Worries
Learning to Trust Our Sovereign God

# GOD KNOWS ALL

God is not leaning over the edge of heaven wondering what the future holds. While Scripture clearly teaches God's omniscience from cover-to-cover, today we're going to examine a text that gives us a specific glimpse into God's foreknowledge and how David responds to it.

## SETTING the SCENE

In the text below, David is on the on the run from Saul while still embroiled in clashes with the Philistines. He seeks God's counsel both on what he *should* do and on what his adversaries *will* do.

## OBSERVE the TEXT of SCRIPTURE

**READ** 1 Samuel 23:1-14. **UNDERLINE** questions David asks God. **BOX** the answers God gives him in response.

### *1 Samuel 23:1-14*

1 Then they told David, saying, "Behold, the Philistines are fighting against Keilah and are plundering the threshing floors."

2 So David inquired of the LORD, saying, "Shall I go and attack these Philistines?" And the LORD said to David, "Go and attack the Philistines and deliver Keilah."

3 But David's men said to him, "Behold, we are afraid here in Judah. How much more then if we go to Keilah against the ranks of the Philistines?"

4 Then David inquired of the LORD once more. And the LORD answered him and said, "Arise, go down to Keilah, for I will give the Philistines into your hand."

5 So David and his men went to Keilah and fought with the Philistines; and he led away their livestock and struck them with a great slaughter. Thus David delivered the inhabitants of Keilah.

6 Now it came about, when Abiathar the son of Ahimelech fled to David at Keilah, that he came down with an ephod in his hand.

7 When it was told Saul that David had come to Keilah, Saul said, "God has delivered him into my hand, for he shut himself in by entering a city with double gates and bars."

8 So Saul summoned all the people for war, to go down to Keilah to besiege David and his men.

9 Now David knew that Saul was plotting evil against him; so he said to Abiathar the priest, "Bring the ephod here."

10 Then David said, "O LORD God of Israel, Your servant has heard for certain that Saul is seeking to come to Keilah to destroy the city on my account.

---

11  "Will the men of Keilah surrender me into his hand? Will Saul come down just as Your servant has heard? O LORD God of Israel, I pray, tell Your servant." And the LORD said, "He will come down."

12  Then David said, "Will the men of Keilah surrender me and my men into the hand of Saul?" And the LORD said, "They will surrender you."

13  Then David and his men, about six hundred, arose and departed from Keilah, and they went wherever they could go. When it was told Saul that David had escaped from Keilah, he gave up the pursuit.

14  David stayed in the wilderness in the strongholds, and remained in the hill country in the wilderness of Ziph. And Saul sought him every day, but God did not deliver him into his hand.

## DISCUSS with your group or PONDER on your own . . .

Briefly recap David's situation.

What is David's first question and God's answer?

What do David's men think of God's answer? What characterizes them?

Do you ever hesitate to obey God because of naysayers? Explain.

---

### ONE STEP FURTHER:

**What outcomes are you wondering about?**
God already knows the end of your story, too. What outcomes do you need to surrender to Him today? Go ahead and write them down.

---

NO WORRIES
Learning to Trust Our Sovereign God

Week Four: **Sovereign Over Everything**

How does David respond in the face of the naysayers?

What happens when David obeys God and goes to battle for the people of Keilah against the Philistines?

What news does David receive while in the gated city of Keilah?

What questions does David ask in response to this news? How does God answer each question?

Does either happen? Why not?

According to verse 14, why wasn't Saul able to catch David? How can this truth bring peace to situations you are facing?

*Notes*

# Digging Deeper

## He Knows You: Psalm 139

God called the rulers Josiah and Cyrus by name not only before they rose to power but also decades before they were even born. He knew what Saul had in mind and what the people of Keilah would do in a politically difficult situation. He also knows *you.* Take some time this week to read Psalm 139 and consider how God knows you!

---

**ONE STEP FURTHER:**

### Word Study: Know

If you have some extra time this week, find the Hebrew word translated *know* and see how it is used throughout the pages of God's Word. Record your findings below.

---

## NO WORRIES
Learning to Trust Our Sovereign God

# GOD GIVES LIFE

## SETTING the SCENE

Hezekiah, King of Judah, was one of a handful of good kings in the southern kingdom of Judah. During his lifetime, Assyria (the world power that conquered the northern kingdom of Israel) came against them. Hezekiah was succeeded to the throne by the worst king of the south, his son Manasseh.

### FYI:

**Sometimes He Says "No"**
David earnestly asked God to heal his firstborn son with Bathsheba . . . but God said "No."

## OBSERVE the TEXT of SCRIPTURE

**READ** 2 Kings 20:1-6. **CIRCLE** references to *the LORD* including pronouns. **UNDERLINE** everything He does.

### *2 Kings 20:1-6*

1  *In those days Hezekiah became mortally ill. And Isaiah the prophet the son of Amoz came to him and said to him, "Thus says the LORD, 'Set your house in order, for you shall die and not live.' "*

2  *Then he turned his face to the wall and prayed to the LORD, saying,*

3  *"Remember now, O LORD, I beseech You, how I have walked before You in truth and with a whole heart and have done what is good in Your sight." And Hezekiah wept bitterly.*

4  *Before Isaiah had gone out of the middle court, the word of the LORD came to him, saying,*

5  *"Return and say to Hezekiah the leader of My people, 'Thus says the LORD, the God of your father David, "I have heard your prayer, I have seen your tears; behold, I will heal you. On the third day you shall go up to the house of the LORD.*

6  *"I will add fifteen years to your life, and I will deliver you and this city from the hand of the king of Assyria; and I will defend this city for My own sake and for My servant David's sake." '"*

## DISCUSS with your group or PONDER on your own . . .

What does God say to Hezekiah through Isaiah?

How does he respond? Who does he call out to?

What does God do for Hezekiah? Is there any indication of why God chooses to heal him? (Be careful; don't jump to conclusions not in the text.)

What about God's defense of Jerusalem? Does the text tell us why He will defend her?

How does Hezekiah finish? Does he use his extra time to set his house in order well? (Finish reading 2 Kings 20 for the rest of the story.)

---

## ONE STEP FURTHER:

### The Life and Times of Hezekiah

If you have some extra time this week, explore the life and times of Hezekiah, King of Judah. What kind of king was he? How long did he rule? How did he finish? What do we know about his son? Use a concordance to locate the information and record your findings below.

NO WORRIES
Learning to Trust Our Sovereign God

## SETTING the SCENE

As God chose to give life to Hezekiah He also gave life to others, some more dramatically. In the text below, Jesus has just arrived at the home of Mary and Martha after Lazarus his friend's death.

## OBSERVE the TEXT of SCRIPTURE

**READ** John 11:32-45 in your Bible. **CIRCLE** references to *Jesus* including synonyms and pronouns. **UNDERLINE** every reference to *the Jews* including pronouns.

### *John 11:32-45*

32  *Therefore, when Mary came where Jesus was, she saw Him, and fell at His feet, saying to Him, "Lord, if You had been here, my brother would not have died."*

33  *When Jesus therefore saw her weeping, and the Jews who came with her also weeping, He was deeply moved in spirit and was troubled,*

34  *and said, "Where have you laid him?" They said to Him, "Lord, come and see."*

35  *Jesus wept.*

36  *So the Jews were saying, "See how He loved him!"*

37  *But some of them said, "Could not this man, who opened the eyes of the blind man, have kept this man also from dying?"*

38  *So Jesus, again being deeply moved within, came to the tomb. Now it was a cave, and a stone was lying against it.*

39  *Jesus said, "Remove the stone." Martha, the sister of the deceased, said to Him, "Lord, by this time there will be a stench, for he has been* dead *four days."*

40  *Jesus said to her, "Did I not say to you that if you believe, you will see the glory of God?"*

41  *So they removed the stone. Then Jesus raised His eyes, and said, "Father, I thank You that You have heard Me.*

42  *"I knew that You always hear Me; but because of the people standing around I said it, so that they may believe that You sent Me."*

43  *When He had said these things, He cried out with a loud voice, "Lazarus, come forth."*

44  *The man who had died came forth, bound hand and foot with wrappings, and his face was wrapped around with a cloth. Jesus said to them, "Unbind him, and let him go."*

45  *Therefore many of the Jews who came to Mary, and saw what He had done, believed in Him.*

---

## ONE STEP FURTHER:

### John 11

You probably know what happened, but it's always good to review. If you have time this week, read the full account of Lazarus's death and resurrection. Record your observations below.

---

## FYI:

### Bethany

Bethany is a village located just outside of Jerusalem.

---

# DISCUSS with your group or PONDER on your own . . .

Describe the situation in John 11:32ff.

How does Jesus respond? What prompts this?

How do the Jews interpret His action?

What did the Jews think would have happened had Jesus arrived earlier? Why?

What does Jesus remind Martha of in verse 40?

What does Jesus pray? Why does He pray what He does?

Week Four: **Sovereign Over Everything**

What happens as a result of Lazarus's resurrection? How does this miracle compare with the miracles people had already seen from Jesus?

Why did God extend Lazarus's life? Did He accomplish His purpose?

Can God accomplish the same purpose in other ways? Explain.

When you face crises, do you consider how God can use them for His glory? How can this change of perspective affect the way you think and act?

*Notes*

# Digging Deeper

## Worriers in the Word: The Kings of Israel During the Divided Kingdom

Last week we compared Saul, David, and Solomon's different worries, the three kings who ruled Israel prior to the division of the kingdom. If you have time this week, consider worry exhibited by the kings of Israel's northern kingdom. Remember, the north didn't have any good kings, just varying levels of bad ones. I'll put some major segments in below and you can take it from there.

Jeroboam — a worrier for the ages.

The "Jeroboams"

The "Omris"

The "Jehus"

---

**FYI:**

**The DyNASTIES of Israel**

Here's a way to remember the big picture of the DyNASTIES of Israel. We'll use the name of the father of each DyNASTY to help us recall the whole group. These are obviously not last names, just mnemonic tools.

**The JEROBOAMs . . .**
Jeroboam (tribe of Ephraim)
Nadab
*COUP* — Baasha (tribe of Issachar) takes over
Elah
*COUP* — Zimri takes over but is almost immediately taken down by the people who raise up Omri

**The OMRIs . . .**
Omri
Ahab
Ahaziah
Jehoram (another son of Ahab as Ahaziah had no son)

**The JEHUs . . .**
Jehu takes over by conspiracy, but God anoints him king
Jehoahaz
Joash
Jeroboam 2
Zechariah
*COUP* — Shallum
*COUP* — Menahem
Pekahiah
*COUP* — Pekah
*COUP* — Hoshea

**THE NORTHERN KINGDOM FALLS TO ASSYRIA IN 722 BC**

---

No Worries
Learning to Trust Our Sovereign God

## @THE END OF THE DAY . . .

As you finish your time of study this week, ask God to help you call to mind the most important truths you've learned over our four weeks together so far. Think on this throughout the day and then record your main takeaway points tomorrow.

## But What About the Enemy?

*Be of sober spirit, be on the alert. Your adversary, the devil, prowls around like a roaring lion, seeking someone to devour.*
—1 Peter 5:8

We've looked at Scripture's teaching about God's sovereignty. We've seen and read for ourselves the truth that God is over all and that the ultimate destiny of every person rests squarely in His hands. There is no rational cause for a Christian to fear death because Jesus defeated death at the cross. These truths are repeated throughout the pages of Scripture.

At the same time, however, we know that God created mankind with responsibility and the ability to choose. He created the angels who serve Him as well as the demons who rebelled against Him. He also created Satan. This week, we'll examine the scope of the enemy's power and assess his threat level to Jesus' followers. We'll also look at biblical directives for standing against him in the strength God provides even when we're tempted to cower in worry or fear.

## SETTING the SCENE

Jesus has just told his disciples that one of them will betray Him. After discussing among themselves who it will be, they turn their attention to the following topic.

**ONE STEP FURTHER:**

**Word Studies: Demanded**

If you have some extra time this week, see what you can find out about the Greek verb that translates "demanded." Very quickly, you'll realize that the particular form of the word only appears in Luke 22:31. Try and locate the root word to see what you can discover both about the specific word that's used and how other forms of it are used in the New Testament. Record your findings below.

## OBSERVE the TEXT of SCRIPTURE

**READ** Luke 22:24-32 and **CIRCLE** every reference to Jesus. In this section they will be pronouns as Jesus is the speaker beginning in verse 25. **UNDERLINE** every reference to the disciples. The disciples are the ones who are disputing in verse 24. Once again you'll be looking for pronouns.

### Luke 22:24-32

24 And there arose also a dispute among them as to which one of them was regarded to be greatest.

25 And He said to them, "The kings of the Gentiles lord it over them; and those who have authority over them are called 'Benefactors.'

26 "But it is not this way with you, but the one who is the greatest among you must become like the youngest, and the leader like the servant.

27 "For who is greater, the one who reclines at the table or the one who serves? Is it not the one who reclines at the table? But I am among you as the one who serves.

28 "You are those who have stood by Me in My trials;

29 and just as My Father has granted Me a kingdom, I grant you

30 that you may eat and drink at My table in My kingdom, and you will sit on thrones judging the twelve tribes of Israel.

31 "Simon, Simon, behold, Satan has demanded permission to sift you like wheat;

32 but I have prayed for you, that your faith may not fail; and you, when once you have turned again, strengthen your brothers."

## DISCUSS with your group or PONDER on your own . . .

What is the disciples' main concern in this section?

Does this remind you of any other texts that we've studied so far? If so, which one(s)? What is the common thread?

How does the disciples' worry compare with the kingdom life Jesus describes?

What practical worries fall away when people don't seek power or status?

Consider your own life. Are any of your worries rooted in a need to control situations or other people? Explain. How can Jesus' example help us obey?

What does Jesus say about Satan and his intent in verse 31?

NO WORRIES
Learning to Trust Our Sovereign God

Week Five: **But What About the Enemy?**

What does Jesus say He has done in response?

If you rest in the truth that nothing can get to you apart from God's knowledge and permission, how will your thinking change? How will your behavior change?

## SETTING the SCENE

Job's name is synonymous with a life of adversity, but his story also showcases the sovereignty of God—even over Satan.

## OBSERVE the TEXT of SCRIPTURE

**READ** all of Job 1 in your Bible. Then, in the excerpts below, **CIRCLE** every reference to *God*, including synonyms, and **UNDERLINE** every reference to *Satan*.

### Job 1:1, 6-12

1   There was a man in the land of Uz whose name was Job; and that man was *blameless, upright, fearing God and turning away from evil.*

6   *Now there was a day when the sons of God came to present themselves before the LORD, and Satan also came among them.*

7   *The LORD said to Satan, "From where do you come?" Then Satan answered the LORD and said, "From roaming about on the earth and walking around on it."*

8   *The LORD said to Satan, "Have you considered My servant Job? For there is no one like him on the earth, a blameless and upright man, fearing God and turning away from evil."*

9   *Then Satan answered the LORD, "Does Job fear God for nothing?*

10  *"Have You not made a hedge about him and his house and all that he has, on every side? You have blessed the work of his hands, and his possessions have increased in the land.*

11  *"But put forth Your hand now and touch all that he has; he will surely curse You to Your face."*

12  *Then the LORD said to Satan, "Behold, all that he has is in your power, only do not put forth your hand on him." So Satan departed from the presence of the LORD.*

---

*Notes*

## DISCUSS with your group or PONDER on your own . . .

Where has Satan been prior to speaking with the LORD?

Who brings up Job in the conversation?

How does God describe Job to Satan?

Why does Satan say Job fears God?

Just so we're clear, what can't Satan do to Job without God's permission?

What does this text teach about the extent of Satan's power against human beings?

NO WORRIES
Learning to Trust Our Sovereign God

How can this truth bring comfort in times of trial or difficultly?

# Digging Deeper

## The Adversary's Tactics

If you have some extra time this week consider how the adversary uses such tactics as fear, doubt, and deception against God's people. Use your concordance to help you locate relevant passages.

What characterizes the adversary's first recorded interaction with human beings in Genesis 3?

What words are used to describe him throughout Scripture? What are some phrases that describe his actions?

What did you learn about his approaches and attacks?

## SETTING the SCENE

With God's permission, Satan strikes Job's children and his property. Job 2 records a conversation between God and Satan in the wake of Job's severe affliction and loss.

## OBSERVE the TEXT of SCRIPTURE

**READ** Job 2:1-10. **CIRCLE** every reference to *God*, including synonyms, and **UNDER-LINE** every reference to *Satan*.

### *Job 2:1-10*

1   *Again there was a day when the sons of God came to present themselves before the LORD, and Satan also came among them to present himself before the LORD.*

2   *The LORD said to Satan, "Where have you come from?" Then Satan answered the LORD and said, "From roaming about on the earth and walking around on it."*

3   *The LORD said to Satan, "Have you considered My servant Job? For there is no one like him on the earth, a blameless and upright man fearing God and turning away from evil. And he still holds fast his integrity, although you incited Me against him to ruin him without cause."*

4   *Satan answered the LORD and said, "Skin for skin! Yes, all that a man has he will give for his life.*

5   *"However, put forth Your hand now, and touch his bone and his flesh; he will curse You to Your face."*

6   *So the LORD said to Satan, "Behold, he is in your power, only spare his life."*

7   *Then Satan went out from the presence of the LORD and smote Job with sore boils from the sole of his foot to the crown of his head.*

8   *And he took a potsherd to scrape himself while he was sitting among the ashes.*

9   *Then his wife said to him, "Do you still hold fast your integrity? Curse God and die!"*

10   *But he said to her, "You speak as one of the foolish women speaks. Shall we indeed accept good from God and not accept adversity?" In all this Job did not sin with his lips.*

## DISCUSS with your group or PONDER on your own . . .

Where has Satan been prior to speaking with the LORD this time?

### There's Not a Demon Behind Every Bush

No doubt about it, once you begin to see the enemy and his tactics, it's easy to fall for the claim of some people that he lives behind every bush and has enough power to thwart every good action.

I've seen people fall for this particular lie and inevitably they are diverted from their focus on the Lord. When they could be adoring Him and His wonderful attributes, instead they are focused on the enemy and his character flaws. It is important to recognize his sticky fingerprints in situations like confusion, bitterness, miscommunication, deception and even drama!

Never forget, however, that you have choices.

We all have choices in relationships, behaviors and ruminations (things we think about). Sometimes it's easy to get caught in the enemy's lies and distortions and just hang there.

So, it's important to see his influence but not to give him credit by blaming him for every quirk in our lives. Our own choices, other's attitudes and life itself can create all kinds of situations and experiences and sometimes it can feel as if we are just victims that have no way out.

He's a defeated enemy who loves to have his way in our world but never forget, "greater is He who is in you than He who is in the world!" 1 John 4:4.

How do God's words about Job compare with His first conversation with Satan?

According to Satan what will cause Job to turn against God?

What additional power does God give Satan over Job? What does He withhold from him?

How does Satan attack Job? How does Job respond?

Again, what can we learn about God's knowledge of and power over anything that comes into our lives?

How can Job's example help us stand?

*Notes*

# Digging Deeper

## God's Power Over the Adversary

Satan may hunt and scheme, but his power is limited. If you have time this week use a concordance, Bible, and Bible dictionary if you have one to identify and study passages related to God's ultimate power over Satan's limited power.

What other names refer to Satan in the Bible? (This will help you identify words to use in your searches.)

What are some examples of God's power over Satan in the Old Testament?

What about the New Testament? Think in terms of the earthly ministry of Jesus and after His ascension.

What truths did you discover that can help you stand against Satan's schemes?

NO WORRIES
Learning to Trust Our Sovereign God

## SETTING the SCENE

Just prior to landing in the country of the Gerasenes, Jesus shows His power over the weather itself when He commands a storm to stop in the presence of His dumbfounded disciples.

**ONE STEP FURTHER:**

### Word Study: Permit/ Permission

If you have time this week, identify the Greek root word that translates "permit" and "permission." See how else Luke uses it in his Gospel and Acts. Also note how it is used in the rest of the New Testament. Record your findings below.

## OBSERVE the TEXT of SCRIPTURE

**READ** Luke 8:26-39. **CIRCLE** every reference to the *man*, including pronouns, and **UNDERLINE** every reference to *demons*, including synonyms and pronouns.

### *Luke 8:26-39*

26  Then they sailed to the country of the Gerasenes, which is opposite Galilee.

27  And when He came out onto the land, He was met by a man from the city who was possessed with demons; and who had not put on any clothing for a long time, and was not living in a house, but in the tombs.

28  Seeing Jesus, he cried out and fell before Him, and said in a loud voice, "What business do we have with each other, Jesus, Son of the Most High God? I beg You, do not torment me."

29  For He had commanded the unclean spirit to come out of the man. For it had seized him many times; and he was bound with chains and shackles and kept under guard, and yet he would break his bonds and be driven by the demon into the desert.

30  And Jesus asked him, "What is your name?" And he said, "Legion"; for many demons had entered him.

31  They were imploring Him not to command them to go away into the abyss.

32  Now there was a herd of many swine feeding there on the mountain; and the demons *implored Him to permit them to enter the swine. And He gave them permission.*

33  And the demons came out of the man and entered the swine; and the herd rushed down the steep bank into the lake and was drowned.

34  When the herdsmen saw what had happened, they ran away and reported it in the city and out in the country.

35  The people *went out to see what had happened; and they came to Jesus, and found the man from whom the demons had gone out, sitting down at the feet of Jesus, clothed and in his right mind; and they became frightened.*

36  Those who had seen it reported to them how the man who was demon-possessed had been made well.

37  And all the people of the country of the Gerasenes and the surrounding district asked Him to leave them, for they were gripped with great fear; and He got into a boat and returned.

38  But the man from whom the demons had gone out was begging Him that he might accompany Him; but He sent him away, saying,

39  "Return to your house and describe what great things God has done for you." So he went away, proclaiming throughout the whole city what great things Jesus had done for him.

*Notes*

## DISCUSS with your group or PONDER on your own . . .

Using your markings as a guide, make a list describing the demon-possessed man.

Again using your marking as a guide, make a list describing the demons.

What did the demons do to the man?

What does Jesus command the unclean spirit to do?

How do the demons react to Jesus?

### Be on the Alert

When God's Word says "Be on the alert," you can be pretty sure that you need to keep your eyes open to what is going on around you.

It doesn't mean that you *will* be caught and devoured by the enemy. It does mean that you *could* be caught by his sneaky ways if you are careless.

Think about people who think they are "fireproof" when they play with fire. Do you think the enemy doesn't love to strike matches of seduction and ungodly behavior around a person who believes he can't be burned?

How many times have I talked with someone who has been caught in immorality who "didn't mean to!"? I can't remember ever talking to someone who said "I really wanted to be seduced and deceived."

Thinking we are impervious to the enemy's tactics is a big mistake. That's the very moment he likes to strike. If you judge another's behavior and think "she is so blind," you may be setting yourself up for getting caught in the same kind of trap as she is in. I always think of the admonition "Therefore let him who thinks he stands take heed that he does not fall" (1 Corinthians 10:12).

Denying Satan's existence or his ability to deceive and draw away even faithful people is a trap in itself. He's waiting, prowling around looking for someone who believes he doesn't exist or at the least believes he doesn't have the ability to take down a saint. Big mistake!

## No Worries
Learning to Trust Our Sovereign God

Week Five: **But What About the Enemy?**

Although there is just one man involved, what does the text us about the number of demons?

What do the demons ask Jesus? What do they need from Him?

What happens?

Think through the implications of this. A host of demons falls at Jesus' feet and cannot act apart from His direct permission. If you are in Christ and Christ is in you, is there any reason for you to fear the enemy? Explain.

## @THE END OF THE DAY . . .

Satan is powerful, but God is omnipotent. Satan is created, but God is Creator. Before you put down your pencil, look back through your week of study and ask God to help you identify the most important truth to help you stand firm against Satan's schemes. Then write it down. If the truth is contained in a specific Bible verse, consider committing that verse to memory.

*Your word I have treasured in my heart, that I may*
*not sin against You.*
*—Psalm 119:11*

# Presumption and the Path to Worry

*So he looked this way and that . . .*
– Exodus 2:12a

Presumption is a push forward that often leads to a pull back. In our zeal to follow God, it's not uncommon to push too far, too soon. Sometimes we confuse our own voice with God's voice. Sometimes we become impatient and try to muscle "God's will" forward on our own power and according to our own time frame. The scenario is played out clearly in the biblical text in the lives of people including Abraham, Moses, and Peter. God still used each of them significantly even after they'd jumped the gun. If you've barreled forward too hard or too soon, you're in good company. One of the problems with gun-jumping, though, is the tendency to become gun shy. This week we'll look at presumption and the subsequent worry it bred in Moses' life.

## MOSES

### SETTING the SCENE

While the narrative of Moses' early days is recorded in the book of Exodus, Luke gives us more of the story in Stephen's Acts 7 sermon. We'll start with the Acts overview and then move back to Exodus.

### OBSERVE the TEXT of SCRIPTURE

**READ** Acts 7:17-25 and **BOX** every reference to *Moses*, including pronouns.

*Acts 7:17-25*

17  *"But as the time of the promise was approaching which God had assured to Abraham, the people increased and multiplied in Egypt,*

18  *until THERE AROSE ANOTHER KING OVER EGYPT WHO KNEW NOTHING ABOUT JOSEPH.*

19  *"It was he who took shrewd advantage of our race and mistreated our fathers so that they would expose their infants and they would not survive.*

20  *"It was at this time that Moses was born; and he was lovely in the sight of God, and he was nurtured three months in his father's home.*

21  *"And after he had been set outside, Pharaoh's daughter took him away and nurtured him as her own son.*

22  *"Moses was educated in all the learning of the Egyptians, and he was a man of power in words and deeds.*

23  *"But when he was approaching the age of forty, it entered his mind to visit his brethren, the sons of Israel.*

24  *"And when he saw one of them being treated unjustly, he defended him and took vengeance for the oppressed by striking down the Egyptian.*

25  *"And he supposed that his brethren understood that God was granting them deliverance through him, but they did not understand.*

### DISCUSS with your group or PONDER on your own . . .

What historical situation was Moses was born into?

Describe Moses.

How long does he live in his father's house?

Who ends up raising him and why? (Answer only from this text or specifically cite other texts.)

What does the text tell us about his upbringing?

What kind of man was he?

What does he do when he's "approaching the age of forty"? Why does he act?

Do his actions make sense to you? Why/why not?

## ONE STEP FURTHER:

**The Women in Moses' Life**
How many women kept Moses alive? If you have some extra time this week, read Exodus 1–2 specifically watching for the women God used to save young Moses' life. Record your findings below.

## SETTING the SCENE

Exodus 2:6 picks up with Pharaoh's daughter drawing Moses out of the Nile River.

## OBSERVE the TEXT of SCRIPTURE

**READ** Exodus 2:6-15, again **BOX** every reference to *Moses*, including pronouns.

### *Exodus 2:6-15*

6 *When she opened it, she saw the child, and behold, the boy was crying. And she had pity on him and said, "This is one of the Hebrews' children."*

7 *Then his sister said to Pharaoh's daughter, "Shall I go and call a nurse for you from the Hebrew women that she may nurse the child for you?"*

8 *Pharaoh's daughter said to her, "Go ahead." So the girl went and called the child's mother.*

9 *Then Pharaoh's daughter said to her, "Take this child away and nurse him for me and I will give you your wages." So the woman took the child and nursed him.*

10 *The child grew, and she brought him to Pharaoh's daughter and he became her son. And she named him Moses, and said, "Because I drew him out of the water."*

11 *Now it came about in those days, when Moses had grown up, that he went out to his brethren and looked on their hard labors; and he saw an Egyptian beating a Hebrew, one of his brethren.*

12 *So he looked this way and that, and when he saw there was no one around, he struck down the Egyptian and hid him in the sand.*

13 *He went out the next day, and behold, two Hebrews were fighting with each other; and he said to the offender, "Why are you striking your companion?"*

14  But he said, "Who made you a prince or a judge over us? Are you intending to kill me as you killed the Egyptian?" Then Moses was afraid and said, "Surely the matter has become known."

15  When Pharaoh heard of this matter, he tried to kill Moses. But Moses fled from the presence of Pharaoh and settled in the land of Midian, and he sat down by a well.

## DISCUSS with your group or PONDER on your own . . .

Describe Moses' childhood from Exodus 2.

Based on Acts 7:23, about how old is Moses in Exodus 2:11?

Compare Acts 7:23-24 with Exodus 2:11-12. Watch the verb usage closely. What additional information does the Exodus account give?

Biblically assess Moses' behavior in Exodus 2:11-12. Did he act properly? Why/why not.

No Worries
Learning to Trust Our Sovereign God

How do Moses' Hebrew brethren respond to his attempt to help them?

**Mixing up God's Will and Mine**

Many times we cause our own worries. I know because I've done it! Several years ago, I took on a project I was sure was God's will. The only problem was the deeper I got into it, the more red flags began to appear. I had presumed that God had given the "go-ahead" because it seemed like a good idea.

The project soon became a problem. It became obvious that it was never God's idea. It clearly was my idea and I had to figure out how to get out of the situation. It brought about losses and emotional pain but it also created worry. How was I going to remedy my poor choice? How was this going to affect other people? How was I going to get back from my wandering path?

Self-imposed problems can be tough but I've learned the best fix is confession to the Lord—confession for the wrong choice and for the subsequent worry. He is full of mercy for His children when we face the consequences of our poor choices and sin.

His mercy (not getting what we deserve) and his grace (his unmerited favor) are available to save us from ourselves.

If you've caused your own worries by bad choices, I encourage you to open your heart before the Lord and lay it all out before Him. He always waits to help when we're willing to ask (Hebrews 4:16).

And don't forget, the good news that He is willing to cause even something you've done that seemed foolish to work together for good, if you love Him. His whole point is for us to love Him. He's a good God who is redeemer even of our messes.

Do you think he expected this? Why/why not? Answer based on the text.

Where does Moses' proactivity land him? How does it affect his relationship with Pharaoh?

Have you ever "killed an Egyptian" because you were tired of waiting on God's timing? If so, how did it turn out?

## SETTING the SCENE

Approximately 40 years pass between the events recorded in Exodus 2 and 3.

## OBSERVE the TEXT of SCRIPTURE

**READ** Exodus 3:1-11. **CIRCLE** every reference to *God*. **BOX** every reference to *Moses*. Remember to include synonyms and pronouns.

### *Exodus 3:1-11*

1   *Now Moses was pasturing the flock of Jethro his father-in-law, the priest of Midian; and he led the flock to the west side of the wilderness and came to Horeb, the mountain of God.*

2  *The angel of the LORD appeared to him in a blazing fire from the midst of a bush; and he looked, and behold, the bush was burning with fire, yet the bush was not consumed.*

3  *So Moses said, "I must turn aside now and see this marvelous sight, why the bush is not burned up."*

4  *When the LORD saw that he turned aside to look, God called to him from the midst of the bush and said, "Moses, Moses!" And he said, "Here I am."*

5  *Then He said, "Do not come near here; remove your sandals from your feet, for the place on which you are standing is holy ground."*

6  *He said also, "I am the God of your father, the God of Abraham, the God of Isaac, and the God of Jacob." Then Moses hid his face, for he was afraid to look at God.*

7  *The LORD said, "I have surely seen the affliction of My people who are in Egypt, and have given heed to their cry because of their taskmasters, for I am aware of their sufferings.*

8  *"So I have come down to deliver them from the power of the Egyptians, and to bring them up from that land to a good and spacious land, to a land flowing with milk and honey, to the place of the Canaanite and the Hittite and the Amorite and the Perizzite and the Hivite and the Jebusite.*

9  *"Now, behold, the cry of the sons of Israel has come to Me; furthermore, I have seen the oppression with which the Egyptians are oppressing them.*

10  *"Therefore, come now, and I will send you to Pharaoh, so that you may bring My people, the sons of Israel, out of Egypt."*

11  *But Moses said to God, "Who am I, that I should go to Pharaoh, and that I should bring the sons of Israel out of Egypt?"*

## DISCUSS with your group or PONDER on your own . . .

What does Moses see when he is out pasturing Jethro's flock?

How does he respond to the sight?

When does God call to Moses from the midst of the bush? How does He address Moses?

What does He tell Moses about Himself?

How does Moses respond to what he hears?

What does God say about His purposes? What does He have in store for Moses to do?

How does Moses respond to God's call? How does this compare with his attitude and actions forty years prior?

# Digging Deeper

## Wisdom Literature Worries

Psalms, Proverbs, Song of Solomon, Job and Ecclesiastes all fall into the category of Wisdom Literature. If you have some extra time this week, see what else you can learn about worry, fear, and the sovereignty of God through the writers of the wisdom literature.

David (Wrote most of the Psalms.)

Other Psalmists

Solomon (Wrote most of the Proverbs, probable author of Song of Solomon and Ecclesiastes.)

Other writers of the Proverbs

Job

No Worries
Learning to Trust Our Sovereign God

## OBSERVE the TEXT of SCRIPTURE

**READ** Exodus 3:12–4:17. **CIRCLE** every reference to *God*. **BOX** every reference to *Moses*. Remember to include synonyms and pronouns.

### Exodus 3:12–4:17

12  And He said, "Certainly I will be with you, and this shall be the sign to you that it is I who have sent you: when you have brought the people out of Egypt, you shall worship God at this mountain."

13  Then Moses said to God, "Behold, I am going to the sons of Israel, and I will say to them, 'The God of your fathers has sent me to you.' Now they may say to me, 'What is His name?' What shall I say to them?"

14  God said to Moses, "I AM WHO I AM"; and He said, "Thus you shall say to the sons of Israel, 'I AM has sent me to you.' "

15  God, furthermore, said to Moses, "Thus you shall say to the sons of Israel, 'The LORD, the God of your fathers, the God of Abraham, the God of Isaac, and the God of Jacob, has sent me to you.' This is My name forever, and this is My memorial-name to all generations.

16  "Go and gather the elders of Israel together and say to them, 'The LORD, the God of your fathers, the God of Abraham, Isaac and Jacob, has appeared to me, saying, "I am indeed concerned about you and what has been done to you in Egypt.

17  "So I said, I will bring you up out of the affliction of Egypt to the land of the Canaanite and the Hittite and the Amorite and the Perizzite and the Hivite and the Jebusite, to a land flowing with milk and honey." '

18  "They will pay heed to what you say; and you with the elders of Israel will come to the king of Egypt and you will say to him, 'The LORD, the God of the Hebrews, has met with us. So now, please, let us go a three days' journey into the wilderness, that we may sacrifice to the LORD our God.'

19  "But I know that the king of Egypt will not permit you to go, except under compulsion.

20  "So I will stretch out My hand and strike Egypt with all My miracles which I shall do in the midst of it; and after that he will let you go.

21  "I will grant this people favor in the sight of the Egyptians; and it shall be that when you go, you will not go empty-handed.

22  "But every woman shall ask of her neighbor and the woman who lives in her house, articles of silver and articles of gold, and clothing; and you will put them on your sons and daughters. Thus you will plunder the Egyptians."

4:1  Then Moses said, "What if they will not believe me or listen to what I say? For they may say, 'The LORD has not appeared to you.' "

2  The LORD said to him, "What is that in your hand?" And he said, "A staff."

3  Then He said, "Throw it on the ground." So he threw it on the ground, and it became a serpent; and Moses fled from it.

4  But the LORD said to Moses, "Stretch out your hand and grasp it by its tail"—so he stretched out his hand and caught it, and it became a staff in his hand—

5    *"that they may believe that the LORD, the God of their fathers, the God of Abraham, the God of Isaac, and the God of Jacob, has appeared to you."*

6    *The LORD furthermore said to him, "Now put your hand into your bosom." So he put his hand into his bosom, and when he took it out, behold, his hand was leprous like snow.*

7    *Then He said, "Put your hand into your bosom again." So he put his hand into his bosom again, and when he took it out of his bosom, behold, it was restored like the rest of his flesh.*

8    *"If they will not believe you or heed the witness of the first sign, they may believe the witness of the last sign.*

9    *"But if they will not believe even these two signs or heed what you say, then you shall take some water from the Nile and pour it on the dry ground; and the water which you take from the Nile will become blood on the dry ground."*

10   *Then Moses said to the LORD, "Please, Lord, I have never been eloquent, neither recently nor in time past, nor since You have spoken to Your servant; for I am slow of speech and slow of tongue."*

11   *The LORD said to him, "Who has made man's mouth? Or who makes him mute or deaf, or seeing or blind? Is it not I, the LORD?*

12   *"Now then go, and I, even I, will be with your mouth, and teach you what you are to say."*

13   *But he said, "Please, Lord, now send the message by whomever You will."*

14   *Then the anger of the LORD burned against Moses, and He said, "Is there not your brother Aaron the Levite? I know that he speaks fluently. And moreover, behold, he is coming out to meet you; when he sees you, he will be glad in his heart.*

15   *"You are to speak to him and put the words in his mouth; and I, even I, will be with your mouth and his mouth, and I will teach you what you are to do.*

16   *"Moreover, he shall speak for you to the people; and he will be as a mouth for you and you will be as God to him.*

17   *"You shall take in your hand this staff, with which you shall perform the signs."*

## DISCUSS with your group or PONDER on your own . . .

What prompted Moses' actions when he was 40? What did he want to do for his brethren?

### Press Hard into God, Tread Lightly Elsewhere

When my first book released the publisher told me that as an author you always have to be pushing your book—always have some in the car, always be ready to talk about it, always be selling. Push, push, push. I tried to but the "pressing hard" and pushing a product just didn't work for me. Sure I sold some books here and there but nothing compared to the effort I was putting in.

So by the time I wrote *Sweeter than Chocolate*, my first study for Precept, I was already a published author and had no aspirations of selling it, no aspirations of "making my mark." I wrote out of obedience to what I thought God was prompting me to do—write a study that would meet the needs of a wide variety of women at my local church. I worked hard, I pressed hard, but I pressed into God's Word and simple service to His people.

The story of how it made it to Precept is a little longer one, but the bottom line is this. God doesn't need us to "kill any Egyptians" to get things moving. He will get His work done on time and better than we can ever imagine. We simply need to follow His lead.

NO WORRIES
Learning to Trust Our Sovereign God

At the burning bush, what does God call Moses to do for his brethren?

According to verse 12, what can Moses rely on this time?

How will this differ from his previous attempt to deliver the people?

Is this assurance enough for Moses? Explain.

What questions and arguments does Moses still have?

How does God respond?

What is the final outcome?

How has Moses changed since his personal exodus from Egypt? Give evidence from the text.

Do you tend more toward presumption (40-year old Moses) or resistance (Midian Moses)? Explain. How can you be more in step with God's call on your life?

# Digging Deeper

## The Need for Realignment

Moses isn't alone in getting out of step with God. Abraham and Peter both had instances of misalignment with God's purposes and timing. If you have some extra time this week, read up on these two heros of the faith examining their lives and God's gentle dealings to realign their thinking and behavior.

### Abraham (Genesis 12–17)

What promise did Abram and his wife "fulfill" on their own? How did God fulfill His promise? How many years did God take to truly fulfill the promise? How many years did Abram and Sarai wait before taking action?

### Peter (John 13, 18–25)

How did Peter's "big words" fall short in the clutch? How did Jesus restore him before He ascended?

What did you learn from these examples that you can apply in your own life?

## @THE END OF THE DAY . . .

Presumptive behavior has a pendulum effect. As we've seen in the life of Moses over-confidence in self is confidence pointing at the wrong object and this can easily swing to fear and worry. This week make it your prayer to live not in self-confidence but in God-confidence that clings to the truth of Philippians 1:6: "He who began a good work in you will perfect it until the day of Christ Jesus."

# God's Strategies for Worry-Free Living

*. . . casting all your* anxiety *on Him, because*
*He* cares *for you.*
−1 Peter 5:7

Because God is sovereign and good, worry-free living is possible but we need to learn His truths and be empowered by His Spirit. Mercifully He doesn't leave us as orphans. God has given us both His Spirit and His Word to help us trust and obey. Will we follow perfectly? Of course not, but by God's grace we walk more and more conformed to His will and ways–the image of His Son.

This week we'll look at some specific biblical strategies for combatting worry and we'll consider the implications of the incarnation in our ongoing battle. We have a God who not only cares but also understands. The incarnation lies at the heart of our salvation. Don't think anyone understands your worry? Jesus does, my friend.

# LOOKING GOD'S WAY

We've read and re-read it, but as we consider strategies to attack worry let's review Matthew 6 one more time.

## Changing Where You Look

What you look at influences where your mind goes.

If you look at a problem and continue to look at it, you see nothing but the problem. When that happens, your behavior will be handicapped, weighed down, intermittently even paralyzed. But there is a solution to this.

We can't deny that there are issues in our personal worlds that concern us. One of the healthiest things we can do is name our worry. "I am worried about _____." And it's really good to linger there a moment to consider whether you can do something about it or not. One defining moment is when we realize we are powerless to change the thing we're worried about. It is then we realize there is only one place to turn.

You turn your gaze to your Father who knows the end from the beginning, the top from the bottom and all the ins and outs. He "knows what you have need of" and He can do something about it.

"My eyes are ever toward the Lord, for he will pluck my feet out of the net" (Psalm 25:15, ESV).

## OBSERVE the TEXT of SCRIPTURE

**READ** the following verses and **CIRCLE** every command to *observe*, *look*, or *seek*.

*Matthew 6:24-34*

24 *"No one can serve two masters; for either he will hate the one and love the other, or he will be devoted to one and despise the other. You cannot serve God and wealth.*

25 *"For this reason I say to you, do not be worried about your life, as to what you will eat or what you will drink; nor for your body, as to what you will put on. Is not life more than food, and the body more than clothing?*

26 *"Look at the birds of the air, that they do not sow, nor reap nor gather into barns, and yet your heavenly Father feeds them. Are you not worth much more than they?*

27 *"And who of you by being worried can add a single hour to his life?*

28 *"And why are you worried about clothing? Observe how the lilies of the field grow; they do not toil nor do they spin,*

29 *yet I say to you that not even Solomon in all his glory clothed himself like one of these.*

30 *"But if God so clothes the grass of the field, which is alive today and tomorrow is thrown into the furnace, will He not much more clothe you? You of little faith!*

31 *"Do not worry then, saying, 'What will we eat?' or 'What will we drink?' or 'What will we wear for clothing?'*

32 *"For the Gentiles eagerly seek all these things; for your heavenly Father knows that you need all these things.*

33 *"But seek first His kingdom and His righteousness, and all these things will be added to you.*

34 *"So do not worry about tomorrow; for tomorrow will care for itself. Each day has enough trouble of its own.*

## DISCUSS with your group or PONDER on your own . . .

What does Jesus command in this section?

What are we to look at? Why?

Have you made peace with this command? Explain.

What truths about God undergird the command? Where else have you seen them attested in Scripture?

Has God been using this passage to change your thinking and behavior since we began our study? If so, how?

**ONE STEP FURTHER:**

**Where are you looking today?**

If you have some extra time this week, pay close attention to where your thinking goes when you're not actively directing it. What grabs the eyes of your mind? What does your mind typically look at or dwell on? Record some thoughts below. Are you satisfied with these, are they pleasing to God, or do you need to readjust your vision and thinking?

NO WORRIES
Learning to Trust Our Sovereign God

# Digging Deeper

## Prophetic Worriers

There may be no job in Scripture tougher than the job of prophet. It's easy to think the prophets had it all together since they worked for God, but even a quick mental survey of the prophets brings to mind those noted for, among other things, whining and crying. This week, if you're up for it, see what you can discover about the prophets worrying in worrisome situations. If you want to look at a worry-free star, spend some time this week being encouraged by the prophet Daniel!

Major Prophets (Isaiah, Jeremiah, Ezekiel, Daniel)

Minor Prophets (Hosea, Joel, Amos, Obadiah, Jonah, Micah, Nahum, Habakkuk, Zephaniah, Haggai, Zechariah, Malachi)

## OBSERVE the TEXT of SCRIPTURE

First Peter focuses on suffering and emphasizes humility and submission in the Christian life.

**READ** 1 Peter 5:1-11 and **CIRCLE** every form of the word *suffer* and **UNDERLINE** every reference to *humility*.

### 1 Peter 5:1-11

1  *Therefore, I exhort the elders among you, as your fellow elder and witness of the sufferings of Christ, and a partaker also of the glory that is to be revealed,*

2  *shepherd the flock of God among you, exercising oversight not under compulsion, but voluntarily, according to the will of God; and not for sordid gain, but with eagerness;*

3  *nor yet as lording it over those allotted to your charge, but proving to be examples to the flock.*

4  *And when the Chief Shepherd appears, you will receive the unfading crown of glory.*

5  *You younger men, likewise, be subject to your elders; and all of you, clothe yourselves with humility toward one another, for GOD IS OPPOSED TO THE PROUD, BUT GIVES GRACE TO THE HUMBLE.*

6  *Therefore humble yourselves under the mighty hand of God, that He may exalt you at the proper time,*

7  *casting all your anxiety on Him, because He cares for you.*

8  *Be of sober spirit, be on the alert. Your adversary, the devil, prowls around like a roaring lion, seeking someone to devour.*

9  *But resist him, firm in your faith, knowing that the same experiences of suffering are being accomplished by your brethren who are in the world.*

10  *After you have suffered for a little while, the God of all grace, who called you to His eternal glory in Christ, will Himself perfect, confirm, strengthen and establish you.*

11  *To Him be dominion forever and ever. Amen.*

## DISCUSS with your group or PONDER on your own . . .

What different groups does Peter address?

### ONE STEP FURTHER:

**Word Study: Anxiety / Care**
If you have some time this week, find the Greek words translated *anxiety* and *care*. Are they related to one another? Where else are they used in the Bible? What else can you learn about them? Record your findings below.

### FYI:

**Strangled and Swallowed**
We saw in the parable of the sower that worry strangles *(sympnigo)* the Word. In 1 Peter 5:8 we read that the devil is literally looking for someone to swallow *(katapino)*.

NO WORRIES
Learning to Trust Our Sovereign God

What instructions does he give each of them?

PAM SNAPSHOT

**Is it fear or is it pride?**

I've always been tightly wrapped. From kindergarten all the way through college I worried about tests. I still remember an answer I got wrong on standardized testing when I was six. I'd worry about homework and competitions and pretty much anything you could worry about.

After soaking in Matthew 6 and 1 Peter 5, though, I've been considering how much of my worry over the years has actually been rooted in pride instead of fear. Certainly plenty has been rooted in fear, but not all of it. I'm grieved to confess that a good part of my worry over the years has been prompted by caring too much about what man thinks instead of what God thinks. Well, that's probably just my issue . . . bet your motives are higher and ways purer . . . Praise God for grace!

Based on your observations and experience, what stresses do pride and self-exaltation bring?

How does Peter describe God's posture toward the proud? Toward the humble?

Are any of the worries in your life caused by underlying pride? Explain.

What is involved in casting our anxiety on God? Make sure you've fully read verses 6-7.

What external threat does Peter address?

How are we to stand against the threats Peter warns of?

If we don't know the Word, can we be firm in our faith? Why/why not?

What does Peter say about God's disposition toward us in verse 7?

What does Peter say God will do on our behalf?

How does knowing God's disposition toward us help us see more clearly in times of trouble?

# ONE STEP FURTHER:

## 1 Peter 5:10 Word Studies

If you have some extra time this week, take a look at what God Himself does for believers. Remember to find the Greek word and use it as the base for your concordance search as you study. Record your findings on the following words.

Perfect

Confirm

Strengthen

Establish

**No Worries**
Learning to Trust Our Sovereign God

Week Seven: **God's Strategies for Worry-Free Living**

## OBSERVE the TEXT of SCRIPTURE

The truth of 1 Peter 5:7—that God Almighty cares for us—is profound. Perhaps even more stunning is that Jesus—God though He is—can truly understand and sympathize with us because while being 100% God, He is also 100% man.

**READ** Hebrews 4:14–5:10 and **CIRCLE** every occurrence of *priest* (be sure to include pronouns).

### Hebrews 4:14–5:10

14  *Therefore, since we have a great high priest who has passed through the heavens, Jesus the Son of God, let us hold fast our confession.*

15  *For we do not have a high priest who cannot sympathize with our weaknesses, but One who has been tempted in all things as we are, yet without sin.*

16  *Therefore let us draw near with confidence to the throne of grace, so that we may receive mercy and find grace to help in time of need.*

5:1  *For every high priest taken from among men is appointed on behalf of men in things pertaining to God, in order to offer both gifts and sacrifices for sins;*

2  *he can deal gently with the ignorant and misguided, since he himself also is beset with weakness;*

3  *and because of it he is obligated to offer sacrifices for sins, as for the people, so also for himself.*

4  *And no one takes the honor to himself, but receives it when he is called by God, even as Aaron was.*

5  *So also Christ did not glorify Himself so as to become a high priest, but He who said to Him,*

  *"YOU ARE MY SON,*

  *TODAY I HAVE BEGOTTEN YOU";*

6  *just as He says also in another passage,*

  *"YOU ARE A PRIEST FOREVER*

  *ACCORDING TO THE ORDER OF MELCHIZEDEK."*

7  *In the days of His flesh, He offered up both prayers and supplications with loud crying and tears to the One able to save Him from death, and He was heard because of His piety.*

8  *Although He was a Son, He learned obedience from the things which He suffered.*

9  *And having been made perfect, He became to all those who obey Him the source of eternal salvation,*

10  *being designated by God as a high priest according to the order of Melchizedek.*

## DISCUSS with your group or PONDER on your own . . .

Who is our "great high priest" according to Hebrews 4:14?

What characterizes high priests in general? What needs to be true of them so they can do their job?

What characterizes their interactions with people? Why?

How did Jesus become our high priest? (Stick to the text.)

According to this text, what did He experience while on earth?

NO WORRIES
Learning to Trust Our Sovereign God

Week Seven: **God's Strategies for Worry-Free Living**

Looking back to Hebrews 4:15, why can Jesus sympathize with our weaknesses?

Because He is not only our God but also our high priest, what does verse 16 call us to do?

How can we apply this when we're overcome with worry, anxiety, or other concerns?

Where is your typical "first step" in time of need? Is it the Word of God and prayer or is it your phone, your e-mail, the checkbook, or something else? What, if any, adjustments do you need to make?

*Notes*

# Digging Deeper

## Meditating on the Word

The Bible is full of exhortations to meditate on God's Words. Take some time this week to see what you can learn about meditating on Scripture. You'll probably want to begin by searching on the English word "meditate" to identify the various original language words the biblical writers use and how they use them. Once you've done your own research, you may want to consult word study helps or commentaries. Record your findings below.

Words translated "meditate"

Who meditated on Scripture?

Why did they meditate?

What benefit did it bring?

How did they do it?

When did they do it?

What is your biggest application point with regard to meditating on Scripture?

NO WORRIES
Learning to Trust Our Sovereign God

## OBSERVE the TEXT of SCRIPTURE

Writing from prison, Paul encourages and exhorts the Philippian church to have the attitude of Christ Jesus.

**READ** Philippians 4:4-13. **CIRCLE** every reference to *God*, including synonyms. **UNDERLINE** everything Paul tells his readers to do.

*Philippians 4:4-13*

4   *Rejoice in the Lord always; again I will say, rejoice!*

5   *Let your gentle spirit be known to all men. The Lord is near.*

6   *Be anxious for nothing, but in everything by prayer and supplication with thanksgiving let your requests be made known to God.*

7   *And the peace of God, which surpasses all comprehension, will guard your hearts and your minds in Christ Jesus.*

8   *Finally, brethren, whatever is true, whatever is honorable, whatever is right, whatever is pure, whatever is lovely, whatever is of good repute, if there is any excellence and if anything worthy of praise, dwell on these things.*

9   *The things you have learned and received and heard and seen in me, practice these things, and the God of peace will be with you.*

10  *But I rejoiced in the Lord greatly, that now at last you have revived your concern for me; indeed, you were concerned before, but you lacked opportunity.*

11  *Not that I speak from want, for I have learned to be content in whatever circumstances I am.*

12  *I know how to get along with humble means, and I also know how to live in prosperity; in any and every circumstance I have learned the secret of being filled and going hungry, both of having abundance and suffering need.*

13  *I can do all things through Him who strengthens me.*

## DISCUSS with your group or PONDER on your own . . .

What does Paul tell his readers to do? Does he repeat or expand on any of his commands? Explain.

---

### Replacing Worry with Prayer

I don't have the worry thing whipped yet. I still struggle. My biggest progress, though, comes as I shift my gaze to Jesus and replace worry with prayer. In fact, I think hard-core recovering worriers are best suited to follows Paul's instructions in 1 Thessalonians 5:17 where he says to "pray without ceasing." The phrase in context sounds very similar to his teaching in Philippians 4:

*Rejoice always; pray without ceasing; in everything give thanks; for this is God's will for you in Christ Jesus.*

—1 Thessalonians 5:16–18

*Notes*

What does Paul teach about God in this section? Where is He? What will He do?

What does Paul command about being anxious? Is there any wiggle room?

What are we to do instead?

What will guard our hearts and minds in Christ Jesus?

What things are true, honorable, right, pure, lovely, of good repute, excellent, and worthy of praise that we can dwell on?

What opposite things do we entertain our minds and lives with?

## ONE STEP FURTHER:

**Word Studies!**
If you have extra time this week, see if you can find the Greek words that describe what we are to think on. Where else are they used in Scripture? What can you discover about each of them? Record your findings below.

True

Honorable

Right

Pure

Lovely

Good Repute

Excellence

Worthy of Praise

## No Worries
Learning to Trust Our Sovereign God

## OBSERVE the TEXT of SCRIPTURE

As we close our week, here are a couple of passages that talk about the importance of keeping God's Word in a place of priority in our hearts and minds.

**READ** Joshua 1:8-9 and Psalm 119:97-104 and **CIRCLE** every mention of *meditate* or *meditation.*

### Joshua 1:8-9

8  *"This book of the law shall not depart from your mouth, but you shall meditate on it day and night, so that you may be careful to do according to all that is written in it; for then you will make your way prosperous, and then you will have success.*

9  *"Have I not commanded you? Be strong and courageous! Do not tremble or be dismayed, for the LORD your God is with you wherever you go."*

### Psalm 119:97-104

97  *O how I love Your law!*

 *It is my meditation all the day.*

98  *Your commandments make me wiser than my enemies,*

 *For they are ever mine.*

99  *I have more insight than all my teachers,*

 *For Your testimonies are my meditation.*

100  *I understand more than the aged,*

 *Because I have observed Your precepts.*

101  *I have restrained my feet from every evil way,*

 *That I may keep Your word.*

102  *I have not turned aside from Your ordinances,*

 *For You Yourself have taught me.*

103  *How sweet are Your words to my taste!*

 *Yes, sweeter than honey to my mouth!*

104  *From Your precepts I get understanding;*

 *Therefore I hate every false way.*

## DISCUSS with your group or PONDER on your own . . .

When are we to meditate on God's Word?

How will it benefit us?

## @THE END OF THE DAY . . .

Take some time to think through what situations trigger worry in your life. Then, look back through the lesson and consider how you can apply God's Word to help you arrest your thinking and behavior to align it with God and His ways. It would be great if you'd record some specific examples below.

Then consider the benefits of meditating on God's Word. How can you integrate the Word into your life and thinking more and more? What are some practical steps you can take? Ask God how you can continue to grow in meditating on His Word and His ways. Then record what you need to below.

NO WORRIES
Learning to Trust Our Sovereign God

## Comforted to Comfort Others

*Blessed be the God and Father of our Lord Jesus Christ,
the Father of mercies and God of all comfort, who comforts
us in all our affliction so that we will be able to comfort
those who are in any affliction with the comfort with which
we ourselves are comforted by God.*
–2 Corinthians 1:3-4

In the worrisomeness of life, God does not leave us alone. He tends us as a shepherd cares for His sheep. He comforts us in our afflictions and in turn calls us to comfort others. If this study has helped lead you to God's healing Words in your struggle against worry, we are grateful and praise God; but we pray that it doesn't stop there. God has put us in community to edify one another–to build each other up, to encourage one another, and to comfort one another as we ourselves have been comforted. If God has comforted you, look around and see where you can share His comfort with someone else.

**Identifying Triggers**

One way God has helped me learn to reduce worry in my life is by identifying worry triggers. I almost hesitate to share this because it is so simple and may seem quite shallow, but alas, I'm willing because I'm sure I'm not alone on this one. Over the course of my life, I've always liked a good medical drama on television. The problem with medical dramas for people bent toward worry, though, is that we tend to "catch" things from our shows. Again, I know it sounds silly, but watching medical shows and reading excessive medical links on-line often trigger worry in me.

Realizing this doesn't mean that I bury my head in the sand and never read relevant medical information or run screaming from every form of entertainment that includes a hospital scene. What it does mean is that I'm careful and particularly on guard when I interact with stimulus that is a known worry trigger in my life.

Your worry triggers may be different. Knowing what they are, whatever they are, will help you better guard your thinking and walk in wisdom and obedience.

Week Eight: **Comforted to Comfort Others**

# THE GOOD SHEPHERD

## OBSERVE the TEXT of SCRIPTURE

Over the past few weeks, we've looked at the power and sovereignty of God over all things, His ability and authority. Today we'll see Him from another angle, an angle that provides comfort in another way. Jesus is the speaker in the following passage.

**READ** John 10:1-18, 27-30 and **CIRCLE** every reference to *shepherd*, including pronouns. **UNDERLINE** every reference to *sheep*.

### *John 10:1-18*

1 "Truly, truly, I say to you, he who does not enter by the door into the fold of the sheep, but climbs up some other way, he is a thief and a robber.

2 "But he who enters by the door is a shepherd of the sheep.

3 "To him the doorkeeper opens, and the sheep hear his voice, and he calls his own sheep by name and leads them out.

4 "When he puts forth all his own, he goes ahead of them, and the sheep follow him because they know his voice.

5 "A stranger they simply will not follow, but will flee from him, because they do not know the voice of strangers."

6 This figure of speech Jesus spoke to them, but they did not understand what those things were which He had been saying to them.

7 So Jesus said to them again, "Truly, truly, I say to you, I am the door of the sheep.

8 "All who came before Me are thieves and robbers, but the sheep did not hear them.

9 "I am the door; if anyone enters through Me, he will be saved, and will go in and out and find pasture.

10 "The thief comes only to steal and kill and destroy; I came that they may have life, and have it abundantly.

11 "I am the good shepherd; the good shepherd lays down His life for the sheep.

12 "He who is a hired hand, and not a shepherd, who is not the owner of the sheep, sees the wolf coming, and leaves the sheep and flees, and the wolf snatches them and scatters them.

13 "He flees because he is a hired hand and is not concerned about the sheep.

14 "I am the good shepherd, and I know My own and My own know Me,

15 even as the Father knows Me and I know the Father; and I lay down My life for the sheep.

16 "I have other sheep, which are not of this fold; I must bring them also, and they will hear My voice; and they will become one flock with one shepherd.

17 "For this reason the Father loves Me, because I lay down My life so that I may take it again.

18 "No one has taken it away from Me, but I lay it down on My own initiative. I have authority to lay it down, and I have authority to take it up again. This commandment I received from My Father."

---

## ONE STEP FURTHER:

### The Lost Sheep

If you have extra time this week, read Jesus' parable of the lost sheep in Luke 15:3-7 paying close attention to what it teaches about the character of the Shepherd. Then record your findings below.

---

### John 10:27-30

27 *"My sheep hear My voice, and I know them, and they follow Me;*

28 *and I give eternal life to them, and they will never perish; and no one will snatch them out of My hand.*

29 *"My Father, who has given them to Me, is greater than all; and no one is able to snatch them out of the Father's hand.*

30 *"I and the Father are one."*

## DISCUSS with your group or PONDER on your own . . .

### Answer based on John 10:1-18

What different types of people does Jesus describe in this text?

How do the different types behave?

What does Jesus teach about the sheep?

Who do the sheep listen to? Why?

ONE STEP
FURTHER:

**John 9 and 10**
If you have time this week, get the whole context by reading John 9 and 10. Pay attention to where Jesus was, who He was talking to and how the hearers responded to Him. Record your findings below.

No Worries
Learning to Trust Our Sovereign God

How does the shepherd call his own? How does he handle them?

## FYI:

### I Go to Prepare a Place

Many of our worries will flee when we're able to view life from the right paradigm. Earth is not our home. Here's what Jesus says about a right outlook on this life in John 14:1-4.

*"Do not let your heart be troubled; believe in God, believe also in Me. In My Father's house are many dwelling places; if it were not so, I would have told you; for I go to prepare a place for you. If I go and prepare a place for you, I will come again and receive you to Myself, that where I am, there you may be also. And you know the way where I am going."*

According to verse 10, for what purpose does the thief come?

Who does Jesus say is the good shepherd? Why did He come and what does He do?

What else characterizes the good shepherd?

Which character in this passage can you trust? Why? What does He provide? (Be sure to include verse 18.)

Answer based on John 10:27-30

According to verse 27, how do sheep respond to their shepherd?

What does Jesus give His sheep?

**The Great Shepherd**

*Now the God of peace, who brought up from the dead the great Shepherd of the sheep through the blood of the eternal covenant, even* Jesus our Lord, equip you in every good thing to do His will, working in us that which is pleasing in His sight, through Jesus Christ, to whom be *the glory forever and ever. Amen.*

—Hebrews 13:20-21

What security does Jesus offer?

Is there any reason this would not be enough for any needs you have?

What fears do you need to lay down?

How can you better align your thinking with the truths of your Good Shepherd's care today?

No Worries
Learning to Trust Our Sovereign God

*Notes*

# Digging Deeper

## New Testament Worriers

Worriers and worrisome situations aren't confined to the Old Testament of the Bible. The New Testament has its share of worriers and worrisomes. As you consider the question of worry in the New Testament, make sure to note any differences you see in people based on the presence or absence of the Holy Spirit.

Synoptic Gospel Accounts

Acts

Paul's Letters

Peter's Letters

Other Letters

John's Writings

Briefly summarize what you discovered and what you will apply.

**FYI:**

**New Testament by Category**
Synoptic Gospels:
    Matthew
    Mark
    Luke
History of Early Church:
    Acts
Paul's Letters:
    Romans
    1/2 Corinthians
    Galatians
    Ephesians
    Philippians
    Colossians
    1/2 Thessalonians
    1/2 Timothy
    Titus
    Philemon
Peter's Letters:
    1/2 Peter
Other Authors:
    Hebrews
    James
    Jude
John's Writings:
    The Gospel of John
    1/2/3 John
    Revelation

NO WORRIES
Learning to Trust Our Sovereign God

## OBSERVE the TEXT of SCRIPTURE

The words of Psalm 23 (a Psalm of David) are so familiar to us that we risk missing its truths. Let's ask God to help us think hard on this comforting psalm through fresh eyes.

**READ** Psalm 23 and **CIRCLE** every reference to the *LORD* including pronouns. **UNDERLINE** everything He does.

### Psalm 23

*A Psalm of David.*

1　*The LORD is my shepherd,*

　　*I shall not want.*

2　*He makes me lie down in green pastures;*

　　*He leads me beside quiet waters.*

3　*He restores my soul;*

　　*He guides me in the paths of righteousness*

　　*For His name's sake.*

4　*Even though I walk through the valley of the shadow of death,*

　　*I fear no evil, for You are with me;*

　　*Your rod and Your staff, they comfort me.*

5　*You prepare a table before me in the presence of my enemies;*

　　*You have anointed my head with oil;*

　　*My cup overflows.*

6　*Surely goodness and lovingkindness will follow me all the days of my life,*

　　*And I will dwell in the house of the LORD forever.*

## DISCUSS with your group or PONDER on your own . . .

List everything the shepherd does.

---

**JAN SNAPSHOT**

### God's Heart for His Sheep

I love the Heart of God that doesn't want us to worry. Just as good parents don't want their children worrying about the family finances or the health of their parents or whether the house is safe from intruders, God, our loving Father doesn't want us worrying about the issues of life.

I learned a long time ago that most things we worry about are out of our control. The statement "There is a God and you're not Him" sums it up pretty well. We can't be God in our own lives or in others'. It's imperative to rest in the fact that we can't fix things that are only God-fixable.

That's really good news to hold on to. Worry is catching. So, if you can just relax and trust God to be God, it will help the people around you. When they see that you aren't going to succumb to worry but are going to rely on God to do what only He can do, you create an attitude of peace around you and that can be catching as well.

Peacefulness and a child-like trust in the face of hard things reflect well on your Heavenly Father. Like children who are well-parented and therefore secure, we are the same. If we recognize how wonderful and faithful our Father is, His security and peace will be all over us and others will see it and be amazed.

---

NO WORRIES
Learning to Trust Our Sovereign God

*Notes*

Now, go back and look at the verbs in the text. What is the object of each of the verbs you listed?

## ONE STEP FURTHER:

**What the Shepherd Does**
If you have time this week investigate some of the verbs associated with the Shepherd more closely.

Makes to lie down

Leads

Restores

Guides

Comforts

Where does the shepherd bring the sheep? For what purpose?

What is the sheep's job?

What needs do the sheep have? What needs do you have?

What threats do the sheep face? What threats do you face?

How does the shepherd provide? Do you trust the Great Shepherd to meet your needs? Explain.

## OBSERVE the TEXT of SCRIPTURE

In 2 Corinthians, probably written on Paul's third mission trip, we see Paul as vulnerable as anywhere in his writings.

**READ** 2 Corinthians 1:3-12. **CIRCLE** every reference to *God*. **UNDERLINE** every occurrence of *comfort*.

### *2 Corinthians 1:3-12*

3 *Blessed* be the God and Father of our Lord Jesus Christ, the Father of mercies and God of all comfort,

4 *who comforts us in all our affliction so that we will be able to comfort those who are in any affliction with the comfort with which we ourselves are comforted by God.*

5 *For just as the sufferings of Christ are ours in abundance, so also our comfort is abundant through Christ.*

6 *But if we are afflicted, it is for your comfort and salvation; or if we are comforted, it is for your comfort, which is effective in the patient enduring of the same sufferings which we also suffer;*

7 *and our hope for you is firmly grounded, knowing that as you are* sharers *of our sufferings, so also you are sharers of our comfort.*

8 *For we do not want you to be unaware, brethren, of our affliction which* came *to us in Asia, that we were burdened excessively, beyond our strength, so that we despaired even of life;*

9 *indeed, we had the sentence of death within ourselves so that we would not trust in ourselves, but in God who raises the dead;*

10 *who delivered us from so great a* peril *of death, and will deliver* us, *He on whom we have set our hope. And He will yet deliver us,*

11 *you also joining in helping us through your prayers, so that thanks may be given by many persons on our behalf for the favor bestowed on us through* the prayers *of many.*

12 *For our proud confidence is this: the testimony of our conscience, that in holiness and godly sincerity, not in fleshly wisdom but in the grace of God, we have conducted ourselves in the world, and especially toward you.*

### ONE STEP FURTHER

**Word Study: Comfort**
If you have time this week, find the Greek word that translates "comfort." You'll be looking for both the noun and verb forms of the word. Then see how else both forms of the word are used by Paul and other New Testament writers. Record your findings below.

## DISCUSS with your group or PONDER on your own . . .

How does Paul describe God?

How many times does the word "comfort" appear in this passage?

What does comfort have to do with God?

FYI:

**Gently Leads**
*He will tend his flock like a shepherd;*
*he will gather the lambs in his arms;*
*he will carry them in his bosom,*
*and gently lead those that are with young.*
– Isaiah 40:11 (ESV)

What does it have to do with us? What does it have to do with others?

What other words are key to this passage? Take some time to mark them and list what you learn about each below.

What affliction did Paul suffer from in Asia according to verse 8?
What characterized it?

Have you experienced anything similar? Explain.

According to Paul, why did God let this happen to him?

What did God show Himself to be according to verse 10?

According to verse 12, what characterizes Paul behavior? How can you imitate this behavior?

How has God comforted you in sufferings and afflictions?

How have others comforted you?

*Notes*

How have you comforted others? How can you comfort others?

## @THE END OF THE DAY . . .

What worries did you bring into this study?

How has God been freeing you of these? What specific truths from His Word have been helpful in your worry battle?

Is there anything you're still struggling with? If so, write it down and ask God to continue to work in your life in this area.

What truth do you most need to remember as you move forward?

How will you keep that truth in the forefront of your mind?

When worry tries to grab you next week, what will you do? What specific steps will you take to walk in obedience?

What is one truth from God's Word that you can actively share with others to help them in their battle against worry?

Take some time to pray and think through your journey with God these past eight weeks and write down your final takeaway lesson below. Then, ask God to cement that truth to your heart and use it to change the way you think and act.

*O LORD, my heart is not proud, nor my eyes haughty;*

*Nor do I involve myself in great matters,*

*Or in things too difficult for me.*

*Surely I have composed and quieted my soul;*

*Like a weaned child rests against his mother,*

*My soul is like a weaned child within me.*

*O Israel, hope in the LORD*

*From this time forth and forever.*

*—Psalm 131*

NO WORRIES
Learning to Trust Our Sovereign God

# RESOURCES

## Helpful Study Tools

*The New How to Study Your Bible*
Eugene, Oregon: Harvest House
Publishers

*The New Inductive Study Bible*
Eugene, Oregon: Harvest House
Publishers

*Logos Bible Software*
Available at www.logos.com.

## Greek Word Study Tools

Kittel, G., Friedrich, G., & Bromiley,
G.W.
*Theological Dictionary of the New
Testament, Abridged* (also known as
Little Kittel)
Grand Rapids, Michigan: W.B.
Eerdmans Publishing Company

Zodhiates, Spiros
*The Complete Word Study Dictionary:
New Testament*
Chattanooga, Tennessee: AMG
Publishers

## Hebrew Word Study Tools

Harris, R.L., Archer, G.L., & Walker,
B.K.
*Theological Wordbook of the Old
Testament* (also known as TWOT)
Chicago, Illinois: Moody Press

Zodhiates, Spiros
*The Complete Word Study Dictionary:
Old Testament*
Chattanooga, Tennessee: AMG
Publishers

## General Word Study Tools

Strong, James
*The New Strong's Exhaustive
Concordance of the Bible*
Nashville, Tennessee: Thomas Nelson

## Recommended Commentary Sets

*Expositor's Bible Commentary*
Grand Rapids, Michigan: Zondervan

*NIV Application Commentary*
Grand Rapids, Michigan: Zondervan

*The New American Commentary*
Nashville, Tennessee: Broadman and
Holman Publishers

## One-Volume Commentary

Carson, D.A., France, R.T., Motyer,
J.A., & Wenham, G.J. Ed.
*New Bible Commentary: 21st Century
Edition*
Downers Grove, Illinois: Inter-Varsity
Press

# HOW TO DO AN ONLINE WORD STUDY

**For use with www.blueletterbible.org**

1. Type in Bible verse. Change the version to NASB. Click the "Search" button.

2. When you arrive at the next screen, click the "TOOLS" button to the left of your verse. This will open the blue "Interlinear" tab.

3. Click on the Strong's number which is the link to the original word in Greek or Hebrew.

Clicking this number will bring up another screen that will give you a brief definition of the word as well as list every occurrence of the Greek word in the New Testament or Hebrew word in the Old Testament. Before running to the dictionary definition, scan places where this word is used in Scripture and examine the general contexts where it is used.

## ABOUT PRECEPT

Precept Ministries International was raised up by God for the sole purpose of establishing people in God's Word to produce reverence for Him. It serves as an arm of the church without respect to denomination. God has enabled Precept to reach across denominational lines without compromising the truths of His inerrant Word. We believe every word of the Bible was inspired and given to man as all that is necessary for him to become mature and thoroughly equipped for every good work of life. This ministry does not seek to impose its doctrines on others, but rather to direct people to the Master Himself, who leads and guides by His Spirit into all truth through a systematic study of His Word. The ministry produces a variety of Bible studies and holds conferences and intensive Training Workshops designed to establish attendees in the Word through Inductive Bible Study.

Jack Arthur and his wife, Kay, founded Precept Ministries in 1970. Kay and the ministry staff of writers produce **Precept Upon Precept** studies, **In & Out** studies, **Lord** series studies, the **New Inductive Study Series** studies, **40-Minute** studies, and **Discover 4 Yourself Inductive Bible Studies for Kids**. From years of diligent study and teaching experience, Kay and the staff have developed these unique, inductive courses that are now used in nearly 185 countries and 70 languages.

 **PRECEPT.ORG**

## GET CONNECTED

**LEARN HOW** you can get involved in "Establishing People in God's Word" at precept.org/connect

*Use your smartphone to connect to Precept's ministry initiatives.*
**Precept.org/connect**

---

**PRECEPT ONLINE COMMUNITY** provides support, training opportunities and exclusive resources to help Bible study leaders and students. Connect at Precept Online Community at Precept.org/POC.

*Use your smartphone to connect to Precept Online Community.*
**Precept.org/POC**

## JAN SILVIOUS

Jan Silvious, an author, speaker, and professional life coach, is known for her biblically sound, psychologically positive answers to women's challenges. A former radio co-host with Kay Arthur for five years, Jan was also a speaker for eight years with Women of Faith®. She and her husband have three sons, two daughters-in-law, and five grandchildren and live in Chattanooga, Tennessee.

www.jansilvious.com

 jansilvious

 jansilvious

## PAM GILLASPIE

Pam Gillaspie, a passionate Bible student and teacher, authors Precept's *Sweeter Than Chocolate!*® Bible study series. Pam holds a BA in Biblical Studies from Wheaton College in Wheaton, Illinois. She and her husband live in suburban Chicago, Illinois with their son, daughter, and Great Dane.

www.pamgillaspie.com

 pamgillaspie

 pamgillaspie

CPSIA information can be obtained
at www.ICGtesting.com
Printed in the USA
JSHW040814260321
12953JS00005B/59